Independent
Walker's Guide
to
Great Britain

Other titles in the series

The Independent Walker's Guide to France
The Independent Walker's Guide to Italy

The
Independent
Walker's Guide
to
Great Britain

by Frank Booth

*35 Enchanting Walks
in Great Britain's Charming Landscape*

INTERLINK BOOKS
NEW YORK

First published in 1998 by

INTERLINK BOOKS
An imprint of Interlink Publishing Group, Inc.
99 Seventh Avenue · Brooklyn, New York 11215 and
46 Crosby Street · Northampton, Massachusetts 01060

Library of Congress Cataloging-in-Publication Data

Booth, Frank W., 1951-
    The independent walker's guide to Great Britain: 35
enchanting walks in Great Britain's charming landscape / by
Frank Booth.
        p.   cm. — (The Independent walker series)
Includes index.
    ISBN 1-56656-295-3
1. Walking—Great Britain—Guidebooks. 2. Landscape—Great
Britain—Guidebooks. I. Title. II. Series.
DA650.B66 1998
914.104'859—dc20   95-20490
                                                         CIP

Printed and bound in Canada
10 9 8 7 6 5 4 3 2 1

To order or request our complete catalog,
please call us at **1-800-238-LINK** or write to:
Interlink Publishing
46 Crosby Street, Northampton, MA 01060
e-mail: interpg@aol.com • website: www.interlinkbooks.com

Contents

Introduction

Part One: Hitting the Trail

1. Before You Leave

2. When You Get There

3. Trail Life

Contents

Part Two: 35 Great Walks

Contents

Cambridge (walk 1)

Introduction

Although this is a walkers' guide, it is also about escaping and avoiding the DROPS. The DROPS are not a communicable disease. They are something far more insidious: the highly-feared DREADED OTHER PEOPLE who are always in your way, going where you want to go when you want to go. You have seen them everywhere—in long lines at the bank, at the supermarket with bounteous baskets standing six deep in front of you, and in disabled vehicles blocking your path during interminable rush-hour traffic. Great multitudes of DROPS are waiting for you in Great Britain.

Seldom will you see a single DROP (perhaps this word can only be used in the plural; a single individual may not qualify for DROPhood). They tend to cluster in large numbers around people who are trying to avoid them. Like stampeding cattle, they destroy everything in their path. International publications are currently reporting the results of their rampaging: as *Newsweek* put it in July 1992, "These days it is tough to find a vacation spot that doesn't in some way resemble a shopping mall, a garbage dump, or a traffic jam."

Even with this book in hand, you will not always be able to completely avoid the DROPS, but you will have a strategy to retain your independence and sanity. For example, if you are sojourning in London, you will want to visit monumental Windsor Castle. In the palace, you will be shoulder to shoulder with DROPS; however, when you leave Windsor do not allow yourself to be herded into a bus or train for an express commute back to London. Take the quick six-mile walk from elegant Maidenhead back to Windsor along the historic River Thames. You will probably spend less time along the trail than you did in line at the Queen's residence, and you will see none of the DROPS whose elbows you encountered at Windsor Castle. You can repeat this scenario at many of the most renowned tourist sites in Great Britain. See the "must-sees," but get off the beaten path and also see the real Great Britain.

This book shows you how to walk between and around sites that are endlessly written about in ordinary guides. The trails described in this book will take you to many of Great Britain's most famous monuments and also to a variety of lesser known but equally interesting areas. You will see the British going about their daily lives on farms, in villages, and along roads too remote to appear on most maps. Local cows, horses, sheep, chicken, and dogs will often be present to greet you.

This book is organized into two sections. The first part, Hitting the Trail, provides all the necessary information for planning your trip: from useful background material on Britain to detailed tips on rambling (the British word for hiking or walking).

The second section contains practical information about thirty-five great walks, including distance, time duration, and a general description of the trail and local sights. Each walk description also has an accompanying set of trail notes and a map that will alert you to possible problems and confusion along the route.

Walking as Opposed to Other Forms of Travel

Why not rent a car or take a train or a bus or even pedal a bicycle? Why walk? There are faster ways of getting around, and if you go faster, you can see more. I understand this mentality and have been on some breathtaking driving tours of Europe, hurtling down expressways from sight to sight at one hundred miles per hour while German cars pass at warp speed. If this will be the extent of your vacation, driving quickly between famous sites, stay home, rent a travel video about Great Britain, and save money.

Although I recommend travel by car, you should also take the time for frequent walks. When you walk, you create unique memories, avoid the DROPS, and seldom see any mechanized form of transportation. All of these are luxuries afforded to few twentieth-century travellers.

Trains and buses in Great Britain are generally very good, and you will want to use these modes of transportation as an aid to your walking. However, I would not recommend spending valuable vacation time riding around on crowded public transportation, particularly during the summer months when the DROPS assemble en masse. When you take a train or bus, you often miss the most important part of your trip—the trail or what lies between your destinations. There are no surprises on public transportation, and you will probably have numerous DROPS and dirty windows separating you from what you came to see: Great Britain.

Some people extol the virtues of bicycling in Europe. Yes, you will get some exercise, and you will see some interesting monuments. You will not, however, get far off the beaten path; bicycles go where cars go—where everyone else goes. The roads that cyclists pedal are less frequented by motorized vehicles but by no means untravelled. Many of these roads are very narrow, almost too narrow for two cars and too narrow for two cars and a bicycle. The traffic in Europe almost always goes at breakneck pace and there is very little reverence for cyclists. Furthermore, European cars are notorious for their choking emissions and high-decibel noise. On a trail, you will encounter none of these difficulties.

The Independent Walker

This book is designed to help you, an independent traveller, plan a walking tour of Great Britain. There is no single way of walking in Great Britain, and whether you are relying on your thumb for locomotion and sleeping in a army-surplus pup tent or leasing a Mercedes to shuttle yourself between multi-starred luxury hotels, you will find this book to be worth more than you paid for it.

All of the walks have been selected according to the following criteria: the walk itself is of great visual delight; the trail is near a noteworthy tourist site or in an area of great natural beauty; there is easy access to public transportation. As an added bonus, all of the walks are along Great Britain's well-known and well-organized system of public trails, where you will always be safe and be able to find your way without becoming lost. Finally, another unique feature of this book is that all of the walks are linear; you will not find yourself walking around in circles (i.e. getting nowhere). Linear walks are interesting throughout their entire length, whereas circular walks usually include a less-than-attractive or repetitious return to the starting point. Linear walks also impart a feeling of accomplishment in having arrived at a town or city in the traditional way of our ancestors, on foot. At York, for example, tracing the path of the Ebor Way you will traverse an ancient landscape, follow the winsome banks of the River Foss, pass through a great city gate, wander along medieval streets, and enter as a pilgrim the magnificent York Minster cathedral. Similar experiences await you throughout Great Britain. You can use a car and public transportation or, if you do not rent a car, use only public transportation to reach starting and ending points. Specific directions are included in the final section for each walk.

In order to plan a remarkable tour of Great Britain consult the comprehensive map on page 6, and look at the suggested itineraries listed on pages 5–20. For travellers with time to burn, there is a comprehensive itinerary, the Grand Tour, which combines all of the greatest sites with a collection of Britain's finest walks. The Grand Tour is peerless as a vehicle for an in-depth discovery of Great Britain.

There are also five regional itineraries: London and Vicinity (especially useful for those with only a few days to spend in Great Britain); The South; Central England/Wales; Northern England; and Scotland. Another unique feature of this book is the inclusion of ten thematic tours: Roman Ruins, Great Castles, Famous Cathedrals, Forgotten Abbeys, Fabulous Forests, High Hills, Beach

Resorts, Coast Lover's Itinerary, Inland Waterways, and the Must-See Itinerary: All the Great Sites. Finally, there are suggested walks for the day before your departure from Great Britain that are close to Gatwick and Heathrow airports (see p. 20).

Although there is a remarkable diversity of tours available to choose from, do not consider this to be a straight jacket. Feel free to construct your own itinerary or combine two or more of the suggested itineraries. In order to determine which particular walks are most attractive for you, inspect the Walks-at-a-Glance section on pages 20–23, which provides capsule summaries of each adventure

Itineraries

The following diverse itineraries are suggested, but feel free to construct your own via consultation with the maps and walk summaries.

The Grand Tour

For the finest tour available in all of Great Britain, complete the following walks in the order presented (1–35). An ambitious, fast-driving traveller could do them all in seven weeks, including four nights in London. For a less frenetic tour, budget about nine or ten weeks.

This itinerary is given in its most compressed form. If you are not on a tight schedule, intersperse your walks with free days to explore each region in more depth or simply relax. Also, on one-night stops you may not arrive in time to make a required public transportation rendez-vous, necessitating an extra day in town; or you may not feel like getting out of your car and going immediately on a walk. Be judicious with available time, and do not push yourself too hard. Remember, you are on vacation. On the other hand it is usually possible for tireless travellers to adhere to the suggested itineraries and enjoy the fast-paced succession of

Itineraries Map

sites and walks. The suggested travel routes are simply the fastest or most direct. Please ignore them, if you have the time, and create a more interesting route along Great Britain's beautiful back roads.

This itinerary, which takes you to a variety of off-the-beaten-path locations, is slightly more difficult via public transportation and may involve convoluted routing in order to reach some destinations. However, for the patient traveller it is possible to arrive at all of the destinations, and I have included information on getting to a destination by train or by a train/bus combination if required. You can get detailed information on connections at any train station and can plan your entire itinerary from London, or consult a more general travel guide to Britain. Finally, the suggestions about where to stay can easily be altered to suit your needs; however, they are generally the most attractive alternative in a given area. I have included no specific lodging recommendations, but the tourist office, a quick ride around town, or a comprehensive guidebook that specializes in lodging will provide you with an in-depth overview of the local lodging scene. Rooms are seldom difficult to find in Great Britain, especially if you are in a car. However, if you are relying on public transportation, you may wish to consult a comprehensive guide book and reserve hotel rooms in advance, particularly in the summer.

Nights 1–2: Cambridge (Walk 1)
From London drive 60 miles (along M11; or one-hour train ride from London's King Cross or Liverpool Street stations) to Cambridge, where there are numerous accommodations in all price ranges. Tour this lovely city on the first day while overcoming jet lag; complete Walk 1 during the second day.

Nights 3–7: York (Walks 2–5)
About four hours north of Cambridge (A14 to A1 to A64 to York; or by train) lies the walled, medieval splendor of York. Although crowded in the summer, York has an abundance of accommodations that can be easily booked at the tourist office. (Alternately, if you prefer beaches to medieval walls, Scarborough offers

numerous accommodations and a fine nautical atmosphere.) Spend night 3 exploring walls and monuments; complete Walks 2 through 5 on the following three days. From York take A59 to A1 to B6265 to Ripon (27 miles) for Walk 3. To Filey and Walk 4 take A64 to A1039 (about 45 miles). Drive along B1363 and A170 to arrive at Helmsly and Walk 5 (about 25 miles).

Night 8 Carlisle/Hadrian's Wall (Walk 6)

In less than three hours you will span the 120 miles between York and Carlisle (A59 to A1 to A66 to M6; or by train), which is a conveniently located base for exploring Hadrian's Wall. If you arrive early enough, Carlisle can be a one-night stand—complete your wall walk in the afternoon and explore Carlisle during evening hours. However, if you are in no hurry, Carlisle is an attractive, historic city with crumbling city walls and a castle built of stones pilfered from Hadrian's Wall; you may sojourn comfortably here for two days or even longer.

Nights 9–10: Edinburgh (Walk 7)

Driving north from Carlisle, you will soon pass into Scotland and within 2 $\frac{1}{2}$ hours (100 miles along A7; or by train) arrive in most edifying Edinburgh, where accommodations abound. Pass day 9 in this stately capital and cultural center (time allowing, at least another day or two would be necessary just to visit the major sites). On day 10 escape urbanism and explore the fascinating Fife Coast (Walk 7) by foot and by car.

Nights 11–12: Aberdeen/Grampian Castle Country (Walk 8)

Three hours north of Edinburgh (125 miles along M90 to A94 to A92; or by train) lies Grampian Castle country and the lovely university town of Aberdeen, which offers numerous inexpensive bed-and-breakfasts (B & Bs) and is an excellent base of operations for castle hopping. Explore the city on day 10 and take Walk 8 on day 11. If you have an extra day, take the 150-mile automobile ride along the Castle Trail.

Night 13: Aberlour/Whisky Country (Walk 9)

From Aberdeen, Aberlour is a quick ninety-minute drive along scenic secondary roads (A96 to Huntly, A920 to Dufftown, A941 to A95 to Aberlour; or train to Elgin then bus to Aberlour). Find a bed-and-breakfast in this comely village (any of the villages in this area are attractive and offer adequate accommodations), revel in the joys of Walk 9, and find nocturnal solitude (tempered by fine whisky in warm pubs) in this most rustic corner of Scotland.

Nights 14–15: Fort William/Scottish Highlands (Walk 10)

About $2\frac{1}{2}$ hours (about 100 miles: A95 to A9, to A86, to A82; or by several trains) from whisky country lies the serrated splendor of the Scottish Highlands, where you will spend two nights amidst the mountain-town ambience of Fort William. Tour the surrounding area and enjoy the town on day 14; on day 15, you will complete the aerobically challenging Walk 10.

Nights 16 and 17: Glasgow/Loch Lomond (Walk 11)

Glasgow, endowed with numerous housing options, lies about $2\frac{1}{2}$ hours south of Fort William (about 100 miles: A82 connects the two cites; or by bus). Here, during day 16, you can tour this cultural capital; on the following day, enjoy lovely Loch Lomond and the land made famous by Sir Walter Scott in his novel *Rob Roy* (Walk 11).

Night 18: Stranraer/Scotland's Atlantic Coast (Walk 12)

Get an early start; drive two hours from Glasgow to Stranraer (A77 all the way; or by train); book a room; take the bus to Portpatrick; walk back to Stranraer along a most magnificent trail; wander about this rugged coastal city; and sleep well—you have had a great day.

Nights 19–20: Keswick/Lake District (Walks 13 and 14)

Keswick, alluringly enshrouded amidst comely lakes and enchanting forests, lies only about $3\frac{1}{2}$ hours south of the urban bustle of Glasgow (about 150 miles: M74 to A74 to M6 to A66 to Keswick; or train to Windermere and bus to Keswick). After booking one of the ubiquitous rooms, take lovely lakeside Walk 13, and enjoy an evening on the town. On the next day tour this lovely region by car and then by foot on Walk 14. A third stress-busting day is not a bad idea.

Nights 20–21: Ribble Valley/Blackpool (Walk 15)

To reach this study in contrasts (Arcadia vs. Coney Island), drive south about two hours from Keswick to Clitheroe (A66 to M6 to A67 to A59; or bus to Windermere, trains to Manchester and then Blackpool, bus to Clitheroe) where you can book a room either in town or somewhere in the region at the tourist office; lovers of the gaudy will prefer the turbulent atmosphere of Blackpool where there are more rooms than grains of sand on a seven-mile stretch of beach. Spend day 20 marvelling at Blackpool's charming tawdriness, and recover on day 21 with most lovely Walk 15.

Night 22: Peak District (Walk 16)

(NOTE: Unless you arrive on a summer Sunday, be prepared to take a taxi to your starting point; also, very difficult to get to via public transportation.)

From Ribble Valley to the Peak District takes about ninety minutes (about 65 miles: A59 to A67 to M6 to M63 to A6 to A625). Here you can traverse rarely trodden land on Walk 16 and spend the night in the remote fastness of Castleton.

Night 23: Northern Wales/Snowdonia (Walk 17)

From very remote peaks to the slightly less remote Caernarfon in Wales takes about 3 hours (about 120 miles: A57 to A560 to M56 to A55 to A487; or by train from Blackpool and then bus to Caernarfon). Book one of the numerous rooms in town, take Walk 17, and wander about town and castle at night.

Night 24: Central Wales/Chirk Castle (Walk 18)

A quick ninety-minute drive from Caernarfon lies Llangollen, which is in close proximity to Chirk Castle (A487 to A55 to A5; or bus to Bangor, train to Chester, bus to Wrexham, and occasional bus or taxi to Llangollen). After booking a room, take the canal-side Walk 18, and then bask in Welsh tranquility.

Night 25: The Iron Bridge (Walk 19)

About an hour southeast of Llangollen (A5 all the way; or taxi to Wrexham, bus to Chester, train to Wellington, and bus to Ironbridge) lies the profoundly historical Ironbridge, birthplace of the Industrial Revolution. Book a room at the tourist office (accommodations are not fully developed in this town but there is always something in the surrounding area), take a walk through the past and be astounded by the local tourist attractions.

Nights 26–27: Wales/Pembrokeshire Coast (Walk 20)

A long $4\frac{1}{2}$ hour drive from Ironbridge will take you to St. David's and Britain's wild coast (about 170 miles: B4380 to A458 to A483 to A470 to A44 to A487; or bus to Wellington, trains to Cardiff, and bus to St. David's). Spend day 26 exploring this most diminutive of British cities and complete exciting Walk 20 on day 27.

Night 28: Wales/Wye Valley (Walk 21)

About three hours from St. David's lies the attractive, adequately-accommodated medieval town of Chepstow with its magnificent castle (about 145 miles: A487 to A40 to A48 to M4 to A466; or bus to Fishguard and train to Chepstow). Here you can take the stunning valley Walk 21 and enjoy your final night in Wales in the shadow of a great fortress.

Night 30: Oxford (Walk 22)

A quick cruise from wild Wales to erudite Oxford (about 80 miles: A48 to A40; or by trains) will result in some culture shock; however, quickly jump out of your car; savor a fine walk down the River Thames; enjoy stately, historic buildings in the afternoon; and imbibe the lively student ambience during the evening.

Night 31: Windsor/Eton (Walk 23)

Just over an hour's drive from Oxford lies magnificent Windsor Castle and its surrounding city with numerous but expensive accommodations (about 60 miles: A40 to M4 to A355; or by train). Book a room; take another fabulous walk down the River Thames;

wander about the Queen's castle; and enjoy Windsor's opulent ambience.

Night 32: Canterbury (Walk 24)
The vehicular pilgrimage from Windsor to Canterbury takes about $2\frac{1}{2}$ hours (about 110 miles: A355 to M4 to M25 to M2 to A2; or by train). Charming Chaucerian Canterbury of cathedral fame, with its excellent accommodations and dining, will probably charm you into a second night, but a tour of the city and the historic pilgrimage Walk 24 can be accomplished in a single day.

Night 33: Eastbourne/Beachy Head (Walk 25)
From historic Canterbury to the nautical result of Eastbourne is about a two-hour drive (about 75 miles: B2068 to A20 to A259; or by train). Book an oceanside room; take the short but spectacular walk from Beachy Head into town; and linger languidly in this fading flower of forgotten gentility.

Nights 34–36: Winchester (Walks 26–28)
Winchester, also of cathedral fame, is about $2\frac{1}{2}$ hours from Eastbourne (about 105 miles: A259 to A27 to M27 to A33; or by train). There are many accommodations; however, they are usually on the expensive side, and budget-minded travellers may want to use Salisbury as a base for these three walks. Day 34 can be profitably spent along the trail with Walk 27 and touring winsome Winchester. On the following two days tour the Isle of Wight (Walk 26) and take the magnificent trek (Walk 28) from Stonehenge to Salisbury Cathedral.

Night 37: Weymouth/Chesil Beach (Walk 29)
Drive 2 hours from Winchester to the sunny (by English standards) oceanside resort of Weymouth (A33 to M27 to A31 to A354; or by train) where rooms abound; revel in the exciting cliffside Walk 29; and enjoy this bustling port in the evening.

Nights 38–39: Land's End/Cornwall Peninsula (Walk 30)
About $4\frac{1}{2}$ hours from refined Weymouth (about 175 miles: B3157 to A35 to A30; or by train) lies pirate capital Penzance, which

makes an excellent base for the spectacularly wild walk from Land's End to St. Just. Spend day 38 wandering about town while avoiding pirates and take Walk 30 on the next day.

Nights 40–43: Bath (Walks 31–33)

From pirates to Roman Bath with its numerous but expensive rooms (both Glastonbury and Wells also make excellent and less expensive bases for these three walks) takes about $4\frac{1}{2}$ hours (about 190 miles: A30 to M5 to A368 to A39 to A4; or by train). Tour this historic and stately city on day 40 and complete Walk 33 along the River Avon the following day. On days 42 and 43, tour Wells and mystical Glastonbury while completing the short Walks 31 and 32.

Nights 44–45: Stratford (Walks 34–35)

From ancient Bath to Shakespearian Stratford is a quick two-hour drive (about 80 miles: A46 to M4 to M5 to A435 to A439; or by train). Book a room; take another great walk down the River Avon; tour Shakespeare's home and town; and spend the evening at the theater. On the following day, tour the Cotswolds and complete your last but definitely not least walk between two of the Cotswolds' finest and most picturesque villages, Chipping Campden and Broadway.

Nights 46–49: London on Your Own

You have just completed the finest tour of Great Britain known to humankind; drive 2 hours to London (about 95 miles: A34 to M40 to A40) and enjoy a few relaxing days in one of the world's greatest cities.

Regional Itineraries

In order to complete regional or thematic itineraries, simply link the appropriate walk numbers from the Grand Tour. Some adjustments must be made in road selections; however, any general map or road atlas of Great Britain will facilitate this task.

London and Vicinity

Excellent public transportation from London to the rest of England makes the following walks possible as day trips:

1: Cambridge
22: Oxford
23: Windsor/Eton
24: Canterbury
25: Eastbourne/Beachy Head
27: Winchester

England: The South

This itinerary includes many of the most popular tourist sites and can be done most expeditiously, particularly if the Cornwall Peninsula is omitted. This is a most excellent and comprehensive itinerary for first-time travellers to Great Britain and can be easily completed in 22 days, including several days in London.

1: Cambridge
22: Oxford
23: Windsor/Eton
27: Winchester
28: Stonehenge
33: Bath
32: Wells
31: Glastonbury
30: Cornwall Peninsula
29: Weymouth/Chesil Beach
26: Isle of Wight
25: Eastbourne/Beachy Head
24: Canterbury

Central England/Wales

Add ten days to your London sojourn for this quick loop through scenic and unspoiled Wales. As an added bonus you will visit some of Central England's most important monuments and hike through some of its most alluring landscapes.

35: Cotswolds
34: Stratford
19: Ironbridge
18: Central Wales/Chirk
17: Northern Wales/Snowdonia
20: Wales/Pembrokeshire Coast
21: Wales/Wye Valley

Northern England

Spend a memorable two weeks in less-visited but no-less-interesting Northern England. Here is a remarkable collection of monuments from England's Roman and medieval past combined with three of Britain's most spectacular national parks and some of the finest scenic beauty anywhere in the world.

2: York
4: Scarborough
5: North York Moors
3: Medieval Past
6: Hadrian's Wall
13: Northern Lake District
14: Southern Lake District
15: Blackpool/Ribble Valley
16: Peak District

Scotland

This wonderful tour of ethereal Scotland can be completed in twelve days from London and covers all of the major regions and both major cities. Scotland's remote beauty manifests itself in wild coastal tapestries, deep forests, serpentine rivers, placid lakes, and savage peaks. This is truly a land to savor, and your memories of its pristine beauty will linger forever.

7: Edinburgh/Fife Coast
8: Castle Country
9: Whisky Country
10: Scottish Highlands
11: Glasgow/Loch Lomond
12: Scotland's Atlantic Coast

Thematic Itineraries

1. Roman Ruins

Some of Britain's most memorable remnants of its Roman past are included in the following walks:

4: Roman lighthouse at Scarborough
6: Hadrian's Wall
14: Roman fort at Clanoventa
33: Bath

2. Great Castles

Some of the world's most romantic and menacing castles reside in Great Britain. If you have always wanted to see Britain's finest fortifications, try the following walks:

2: York (fortified city)
3: Scarborough (Scarborough Castle)
5: North York Moors (Helmsley Castle)
7: Edinburgh (Edinburgh Castle)
8: Castle Country (Dunnotar Castle)
15: Blackpool/Ribble Valley (Clitheroe Castle)
16: Peak District (Peveril Castle)
17: Northern Wales/Snowdonia (Caernarfon Castle)
18: Central Wales (Chirk Castle)
21: Wales/Wye Valley (Chepstow Castle)
23: Windsor/Eton (Windsor Castle)

3. Famous Cathedrals

Great Britain is noted for the beauty of its cathedrals. The following walks terminate at one of Britain's most famous cathedrals:

2: York (York Minster)
3: Ripon/Fountains Abbey (Ripon Cathedral)
20: Pembrokeshire Coast (St. David's Cathedral)
24: Canterbury (Canterbury Cathedral)
27: Winchester (Winchester Cathedral)
28: Salisbury (Salisbury Cathedral)
32: Wells (Wells Cathedral)

4. Forgotten Abbeys

The haunting loneliness and pacific tranquility of the Middle Ages is most easily evoked at an abandoned abbey. The following walks will take you into these treasures of the past and back to the Middle Ages:

3: Ripon/Fountains Abbey (Fountains Abbey)
5: North York Moors (Rievaulx Abbey)
15: Ribble Valley/Blackpool (Sawley Abbey)
19: Ironbridge (Buildwas Abbey)
21: Wales/Wye Valley (Tintern Abbey)
31: Glastonbury (Glastonbury Abbey)

5. Fabulous Forests

Although England has been largely deforested throughout the centuries, many large and verdant woodlands still exist. The following walks will take you into a world of leafy solitude:

3: Ripon/Fountains Abbey
5: North York Moors
9: Whisky Country
11: Glasgow/Loch Lomond
13: Northern Lake District

21: Wales/Wye Valley
35: Cotswolds

6. High Hills

Although most of the walks in this book are fairly easy, if you are looking for the most aerobically challenging routes, try the following:

6: Hadrian's Wall
10: Scottish Highlands
12: Scotland's Atlantic Coast
16: Peak District
30: Land's End
32: Wells

7. Beach Resorts

Although sunny skies seldom hover long over Great Britain, there are numerous beach resorts that still cater to those who do not have the time, money, or inclination to travel into the perils of southern Europe or beyond. They are usually quite interesting from an historic and architectural point of view. The low-brow entertainment available in many of these places also rates highly as a cultural experience. The following walks take you into this arcane world known to few foreign tourists:

4: Scarborough (Scarborough and Filey beaches)
15: Blackpool/Ribble Valley (Blackpool)
25: Eastbourne/Beachy Head
26: Isle of Wight (Ryde)
29: Weymouth/Chesil Beach

8. Coast Lover's Itinerary

The following walks take full advantage of Britain's stunningly beautiful coastal scenery:

4: Scarborough to Filey

7: Fife Coast/Edinburgh

8: Dunnotar Castle

12: Scotland's Atlantic Coast

20: Pembrokeshire Coast

25: Eastbourne/Beachy Head

29: Weymouth/Chesil Beach

30: Land's End/Cornwall Peninsula

9. Inland Waterways

The following trails follow, at least partially, the course of Britain's beautiful lakes, rivers, and canals:

2: Strensall to York (River Foss)

9: Whisky Country (River Spey)

11: Glasgow/Loch Lomond

12: Northern Lake District (Derwent Water)

15: Blackpool/Ribble Valley (River Ribble)

18: Central Wales/Chirk Castle (Shropshire Union Canal)

19: Ironbridge (River Severn)

21: Wales/Wye (River Wye)

22: Oxford (River Thames)

23: Windsor/Eton (River Thames)

27: Winchester (River Itchen)

33: Bath (River Avon)

34: Stratford (River Avon)

10. Must-See Itinerary: All the Great Sights

If you have a limited time in England and wish to see the most famous sights while enjoying a good walk, choose from among the following:

1: Cambridge

2: York

6: Hadrian's Wall

7: Edinburgh/Fife Coast

Airport Departure Walks

A good way to avoid London traffic on the day of your departure from England is to stay at Windsor the night before a Heathrow departure and complete Walk 23, or stay at Eastbourne the night before a Gatwick departure and complete Walk 25.

Walks-at-a-Glance

These brief summaries will help you decide which itinerary is best for you or allow you to assemble your own unique itinerary. Details for each walk can be found in Part Two.

Walk 1   **Cambridge:** *Kingston to Cambridge via the Wimpole Way*
Savor a wonderful walk through scenic Cambridgeshire, traversing several quaint villages, fertile fields, and the Cambridgeshire and Isle of Ely Naturalist Trust Nature Reserve, inhabited by numerous species of birds and wildlife. Arrive through the back door of historic Cambridge with plenty of time to tour the architectural masterpieces, take a punt ride down the River Cam, and imbibe the lively student atmosphere.

Walk 2   **York:** *Strensall to York via the Ebor Way*
Cross the oxymoronic, vintage-1798 New Bridge at Strensall and follow the winsome banks of the River

Foss into York, one of England's best-preserved medieval cities. Along the way, you will view England's change from a primarily rural to a suburban nation. You will enter York through imposing Monk Gate, scurry along narrow shop-filled streets, and be stunned by the enormity of the city's great cathedral. You can get no closer to the Middle Ages.

Walk 3 **Medieval Past:** *Ripon Cathedral to Fountains Abbey*
Ripon, nestled around a two-acre market place, has almost forgotten the twentieth century, and still employs a man to sound the horn signalling the night-watch. Visit the twelfth-century cathedral before embarking along a medieval track to Fountains Abbey, the most complete and spectacular abbatial ruins in all of Great Britain. Along the way, you will pass through remote, one-street hamlet Studley Roger, a deep forest, and the extensive grounds of Studley Royal, harboring England's most elaborate water gardens.

Walk 4 **North Sea:** *Scarborough to Filey via the Cleveland Way*
Parsley, sage, rosemary, and thyme: Scarborough Fair, famous during the Middle Ages, is yours to enjoy as well as lovely beaches, and a medieval castle harboring a Roman lighthouse. Trek southward along the rugged North Sea coast, passing concrete bunkers designed to ward off Nazi invasions during World War II. Your destination, Filey, is an unparalleled cultural experience: a working-class, carnival-like beach resort—muscle shirts and tattoos are everywhere and on both sexes.

Walk 5 **North York Moors:** *Helmsley Castle to Rievaulx Abbey via the Cleveland Way*

Here in one of England's largest remaining expanses of wilderness, North York Moors National Park, you will saunter quickly between two remarkable sites: Helmsley Castle, a most romantic ruin, which still looms ominously over its town, and the well preserved ruins of Rievaulx Abbey hidden in the shadows of the pristine Rye Valley. The path makes a lovely transition from serene rolling pastures to a forested world of verdant luminosity which at times becomes as dense as a rainforest.

Walk 6 **Roman Heritage:** *Hadrian's Wall via the Penine Way*

Walk along one of Britain's finest monuments, a great wall built by the Emperor Hadrian during the second century A.D. to keep Celtic barbarians from despoiling Roman civilization to the south. You will course several of the best preserved miles while enjoying unparalleled views in all directions. Ponder the passage of time and watch out for the barbarians!

Walk 7 **Edinburgh/Fife Coast:** *Crail to Pittenweem via the Fife Coast Walk*

A stone's throw from Edinburgh lies the unspoiled Fife Coast, where fishing, not tourism, is still the local economic engine. You will walk along the sea coast through three of the finest fishing villages in Great Britain and one of the most commodious pig farms in the world. Enjoy the nautical ambience as you explore ancient harbors, traverse a placid shoreline, and peer into azure blue waters.

Walk 8   **Scotland's Castle Country:** *Stonehaven to Dunnotar Castle*

The area around Aberdeen is Scotland's castle country, and if you become castle weary you may stop at one of the numerous regional distilleries for a relaxing tour and drink. Do not miss Dunnotar Castle, set for Franco Zefferelli's film *Hamlet*. The castle is perched ominously above the crashing waves of the North Sea, surrounded by sheer cliffs on three sides. Today's walk, with mysterious Dunnotar Castle almost always in view, is nothing short of spectacular. The tour of the ruins is equal to the walk, making this a stop not to be missed on any trip to Great Britain.

Walk 9   **Scotland's Whisky Country:** *Dufftown to Aberlour via the Speyside Way*

This is a riverside walk in Scotland's whisky country, first following the course of an abandoned railway line along the fast moving River Fiddich and then coursing the banks of the wide River Spey. In less than two hours, visit three of Scotland's finest small towns; stop for lunch midway at the arch-traditional, riverside Hotel Craigellachie; ramble past fly fishermen hip deep in swift waters; pass through a most menacing (in appearance only) nineteenth-century railway tunnel; and enjoy some of the finest green-valley scenery available anywhere.

Walk 10   **Scottish Highlands:** *Altnafeadh to Kinlochleven via the West Highland Way*

The Scottish Highlands embody the ideal of rugged beauty—serrated peaks, tempestuous coastal terrain, and often ethereal loneliness. Today, an aerobic thirty-minute hike up the appropriately named Devil's Staircase leads to a world of hidden lakes, startling vistas, and remote mountain trails. This is the area described by Robert Louis Stevenson in *Kidnapped*, and there is no finer walk in the Scottish Highlands.

Walk 11   Glasgow/Loch Lomond: *Ardlui to the Drover's Inn at Inverarnan via the West Highland Way*

Take a walk along one of Britain's largest and most beautiful lakes—the world immortalized by Sir Walter Scott in his novel *Rob Roy*. From placid Ardlui on the shores of Loch Lomond ferry across to the roadless east shore; traverse rolling, lakeside hills; trace the course of the swift-moving River Falloch; and drink heartily at the Drover's Inn, established 1701 and still waiting to be remodelled. No trip to Glasgow is complete without this excursion.

Walk 12   South Scotland's Atlantic Coast: *Portpatrick to Stranraer via the Southern Upland Way*

Walk between the tiny, untouristed fishing village of Portpatrick and Stranraer, a major port and home of the ferry to Northern Ireland. This long but varied trek begins along high cliffs overlooking the Atlantic Ocean, turns inland at a working lighthouse, passes through remote farmland, skirts a small lake, and traverses an extensive moor region. An extra day in Scotland would be well spent here.

Walk 13   Northern Lake District: *Grange to Keswick via the Cumbria Way*

Follow the shores of lovely Derwent Water in England's largest national park. From the tranquil village of Grange, climb to the high country that skirts Derwent Water, one of England's most beautiful lakes.

Descending from the hills you will enter a shimmering, emerald-green forest and follow secluded woodland paths into one of the Lake District's most attractive and commodious towns, Keswick.

Walk 14   Southern Lake District: *Ravenglass to Muncaster Mill*

Take a ride on a miniature steam train; arrive at Ravenglass (former Roman port of Clanoventa), and visit the railway museum; walk along a woodland trail to Walls Castle, the tallest Roman ruin in Great Britain; continue along to Muncaster Castle, where you may tour the park-line grounds, visit one of the largest owl collections in the world, and inspect the castle interior (former home of Thomas Skelton of the word "tomfoolery" fame), inhabited since the thirteenth century; finally, you will end this mini-adventure at the still functioning Muncaster Mill, where flour was first ground in 1455. It is difficult to imagine a more eventful four-mile walk.

Walk 15   Ribble Valley/Blackpool: *Sawley Abbey to Clitheroe via the Ribble Way*

Visit Blackpool, Britain's Coney Island, but sojourn in the pacific and proximate Ribble Valley. Inspect the ruins of diminutive Sawley Abbey; stride through the remote town of Sawley, competing with geese for the right-of-way; perambulate through a rolling green countryside tracing the course of a most beautiful river; and arrive a couple of hours later at Clitheroe with more than enough time to inspect castle ruins and enjoy the ambience of this fine town.

Walk 16   Peak District: *Miller's Dale to Castleton via the Limestone Way*
Explore one of England's largest national parks and take one of the finest walks available in this outdoorsperson's paradise. Linger briefly at quaint Miller's Dale, along the banks of the River Wye, before entering into a world of undulating terrain, incisor-like gray hills, barren pasturelands, stone-walled paths, woodlands, and an occasional isolated village. At walk's end, you will be rewarded by a visit to Peveril Castle, built by William the Conqueror's bastard son, and a brief (perhaps overnight) sojourn in accommodating Castleton.

Walk 17   Northern Wales/Snowdonia: *Groeslon to Caernarfon Castle via the Lon Eifion*
Stroll along a path sheltered by dense stands of deciduous trees and graced with an effusion of wild flowers. Enjoy glances at the great tides of the Atlantic Ocean while observing the poverty of rural Wales. Amble into Welsh-speaking Caernarfon, awestruck by the views of the enormous Caernarfon Castle. This short but eventful walk makes an excellent introduction to the joys of Wales and provides the opportunity to visit one of Britain's finest castles.

Walk 18   Central Wales: *Chirk to Llangollen via the Shropshire Union Canal/Offa's Dyke*
Visit unique Chirk Castle, inhabited since its construction almost 700 years ago; walk through a lengthy abandoned canal tunnel and into a shimmering emerald-green valley; cross a towering viaduct; and enter the Welsh outdoor-sport capital of Llangollen, where you may linger long in a café or visit the twelfth-century castle perched high above the town.

Walk 19   **Ironbridge:** *Buildwas Abbey to Ironbridge*
Today's time trek begins in the remote medieval past
and, within a couple miles, passes to the dawn of
the modern age. All of this takes place within the
sobering shadow of a nuclear power plant, emphasizing our remoteness from not only the Middle Ages
but also from the last century. This short but eventful riverside walk takes you from twelfth-century
Buildwas Abbey to Ironbridge, birthplace of the Industrial Revolution. The experiments performed here
by Abraham Darby revolutionized the iron industry,
making it possible for iron to be used for wheels,
rails, steam engines, locomotives, ships, and Ironbridge's eponymous iron bridge (the world's first, built
in 1776 and still standing).

Walk 20   **Wales/Pembrokeshire Coast:** *Solva to St.
David's via the Pembrokeshire Coast Path*
This is an exhilarating adventure in which you will
survey some of Britain's most stunning coastal scenery.
Wind, waves, and sea gulls will be your constant
companions—a wonderfully wild afternoon. St.
David's is worthy of the preceding walk. Home of a
magnificent cathedral, this elfin city enchants visitors
with its peninsular loneliness and welcoming atmosphere. Spend the night or a week.

Walk 21   **Wales/Wye Valley:** *Tintern Abbey to
Chepstow Castle via the Wye Valley Walk*
Trek between two of Wales' most magnificent medieval sites, Tintern Abbey and Chepstow Castle. After visiting the abbey's impressive ruins, slip quietly
into a green forested seclusion and hike through an
undulating, pristine landscape along the serpentine
River Wye. Your destination, imposing Chepstow

Castle, awaits on its lofty perch. Enjoy castle views available only to the foot-propelled and enter the castle gate as a medieval traveller.

Walk 22 **Oxford:** *Radley to Oxford via the Thames River Walk*
Oxford, city of inspiring spires, enchants by the antiquity of its elevated, erudite, and edifying ambience. However, this trek down the River Thames is the highlight of any visit Oxford. Fishermen recline lazily along the banks, and pleasure craft ply the placid waters alongside graceful swans. As you approach Oxford, the Thames becomes a playground for athletically inclined academics: walkers, joggers, and cyclists strive for ascendancy along grassy banks while others sail or row through serried waters.

Walk 23 **Windsor/Eton:** *Maidenhead to Windsor/Eton via the Thames River Walk*
Another stroll down the regal River Thames that takes you from opulent Maidenhead's downtown shopping district through elegant Eton (where you may spot a future prime minister rowing down the Thames) to the pomp and circumstance of Windsor Castle, largest inhabited fortress in the world. The trail views of the castle are astonishing and available only to the pedestrian.

Walk 24 **Canterbury:** *Chilham Castle to Canterbury Cathedral via the North Downs Way/Pilgrims' Way*
Follow an ancient pilgrimage route to one of England's most venerable and bloody cathedrals, site of Thomas à Becket's murder, while dreaming of a lost Chaucerian world. You will begin at the almost unique

octoganal twelfth-century Chilham Castle and pass through a medieval landscape of carefully cultivated fields, verdant forests, and thatched-roofed villages. Approaching Canterbury, the views of the cathedral, fortress, and medieval walls are unparalleled.

Walk 25 **Eastbourne:** *Beachy Head to Eastbourne via the South Downs Way*

Close to London and Gatwick Airport, save this short walk for the day before your Gatwick departure. Eastbourne, home of the nineteenth-century leisure class, is the terminus for this remarkable oceanside walk. Begin at the diminutive Beachy Head lighthouse perched 500 feet above the clamorous sea and trek along high cliffs into lively Eastbourne filled with city-sick Londoners seeking breathable air and respite from strident street sounds.

Walk 26 **Isle of Wight:** *Seaview to Ryde via the Isle of Wight Coastal Path*

Today you will have the opportunity to visit an Atlantic island via a swift ferry, walk a fantastic three oceanside miles, and enjoy the tranquil ambiance of a remarkable seaside resort. The Isle of Wight, often called "England in miniature," is still the haven of yachtsmen, but less-than-patrician types, including walkers, have discovered this pacific Atlantic gem. If you have enough time, spend a couple of days here; walking/exploration opportunities abound.

Walk 27 **Winchester:** *Shawford to Winchester Cathedral via the Itchen Way*

Today's walk takes you down a remote rural river, up an ancient fortified hill, and into famous Winchester Cathedral. From the archetypal sleepy English village of Shawford, you will follow the Itchen, a slow moving, shallow sliver of a river whose flora encroaches from all directions threatening leafy strangulation. Having taken a short detour to St. Catherine's Hill, home of Iron Age settlers, you will bound quickly into bustling Winchester, bursting with medieval monuments.

Walk 28   **Stonehenge/Salisbury:** *Stonehenge to Salisbury (Old Sarum) via the Wessex Way*
Marvel at Stonehenge's mysterious megaliths. Were stones really transported from Ireland and erected by Merlin's magic powers or constructed by a race of extinct giants? Ponder these questions and more as you perambulate through the mysterious beauty of the Salisbury Plain and course along the swift-moving River Avon until you reach the medieval ghost town of Old Sarum, originally an Iron Age fortification of Olympian proportions and more recently the thirteenth-century predecessor of Salisbury. From Old Sarum you are only a short walk or bus ride from Salisbury, home of one of England's finest cathedrals and numerous other remnants of the Middle Ages.

Walk 29   **Weymouth/Chesil Beach:** *Portland Bill to Chesil via the Southwest Coastal Path*
Portland Bill is the southern tip of the Isle of Portland, where a lonely (except for day tourists) lighthouse guides sailors away from lofty cliffs. Climb to the top for astonishing views; stop at the proximate café; and quickly embark upon the trail. Five minutes away from the lighthouse, you will begin a memorable walk along sheer cliffs with immense views

of the Atlantic Ocean and sandy beaches far below. Chesil, your goal, sits snugly along a tranquil bay and makes an excellent place for an overnight sojourn. If you prefer a more bustling atmosphere, unpack at Weymouth, one of England's busiest oceanside resorts.

Walk 30 **Cornwall Peninsula:** *Land's End to St. Just via the Southwest Coastal Path*
The appropriately named Land's End marks England's western extremity. Here at this site of ethereal beauty an amusement-park atmosphere has co-opted the peace and tranquility that should reign. Have a brief, tawdry, and amusing fling before climbing out of Land's End and onto vertiginous cliffs en route to picturesque St. Just. Along the way you will traverse sandy beaches, circumambulate rocky coves, and visit the site of King Arthur's victory over bloodthirsty Danish invaders.

Walk 31 **Glastonbury:** *Over the Tor and into Glastonbury via the Somerset Way*
Glastonbury is the tie-dye capital of England, a mecca for "New Age Travellers" (modern-day British hippies). Any unorthodox garb is acceptable here, and Merlin himself in full magician's regalia could stroll city streets unnoticed. The connection to Merlin is not casual, since Glastonbury is the center of the Arthurian legend. According to tradition, King Arthur is buried in Glastonbury Abbey; the Chalice Well is the location of the Holy Grail; and your walk over the Tor will put you on top of the Isle of Avalon. It is also claimed that Jesus travelled here, and Joseph

of Arimathea built England's first Christian church on the site of the abbey.

Walk 32 **Wells:** *Wookey Hole to Wells via the West Mendip Way*

Wookey Hole (not Chewbacca's birthplace) is a peculiar patina of glossy commercialism combined with items of genuine interest. Visit "Britain's Most Spectacular Caves," edify yourself at England's last handmade paper mill, and inspect a museum that looks like a set from a Fellini movie. Climb out of town and onto a deeply forested hill. At the summit, you will be rewarded by outstanding views of Wells, your destination, and the distant Tor, home of the legendary Isle of Avalon. Stroll downhill into Wells, one of England's most diminutive but also most attractive cities. The town stands in medieval compactness around its star attraction, the Cathedral Church of St. Andrew. Visit the cathedral, tour the other buildings of the cathedral complex, and enjoy the comfortable ambience of this pacific patch of urbanity.

Walk 33 **Bath:** *Saltford to Bath via the Avon Walkway*

The Romans established England's first spa resort here, building an extensive system of baths and ancillary structures. Today these Roman ruins justifiably attract throngs of visitors who also fill the opulent streets of this unusually elegant city. Bath's most engaging and least touristed attribute is the River Avon. Today, you will parallel this venerable waterway for several miles through quintessential English countryside and enter Bath along its nineteenth-century industrial corridor, where ancient factories still loom precipitously over the river.

Walk 34   **Stratford:** *Welford-on-Avon to Stratford via the Avon Valley Footpath*
No city has profited more from the birth of a single citizen. Stratford is a single-industry town: Shakespeare is everywhere. You can visit Shakespearian sites ad nauseum and see the finest productions of Shakespeare's plays in the world, but a walk down the River Avon will take you to the land that Shakespeare knew; he would not recognize the city that has grown around his house. See the sites early before the arrival of tourist buses; stroll through Shakespeare's countryside in the afternoon; and enjoy a world-class Shakespearian production in the evening—a totally satisfying Shakespearian sojourn.

Walk 35   **Cotswolds:** *Chipping Campden to Broadway via the Cotswold Way*
Stunning honey-hued stone combined with artful architecture has produced the Cotswold villages of Elysian beauty set in an emerald arcadia worthy of Oz. In this land that time forgot, you will trek between two most beautiful villages and pause along the way at towering eighteenth-century Broadway Tower for multi-miled views in all directions. This walk represents rustic charm at its most picturesque.

Part One
Hitting the Trail

1. Before You Leave

Other Travel Guides

The stolidly written but very useful green Michelin Guides provide a good general overview of Great Britain. There is a single book that covers all of Great Britain and also two regional guides. Each has a map in the front that rates the importance of all the sites, major and minor, within a certain region. They also have sections relating to history, culture, and specific monuments. I am often surprised to find even the most obscure places mentioned and do not hesitate to consult these guides when I am formulating walking and driving routes. They can be purchased in many bookstores and are moderately priced.

When my wife purchased a *Let's Go: Europe* book in 1985, I humored her by saying that it was a good idea. What I actually thought was that it was a waste of money, and I had nothing to learn from a cabal of callow college students. Before going to Europe that summer I deigned to regard only the book's covers, shunning the contents. Slowly, while driving, as my wife continued to stridently bark out many useful bits of information, I was converted. At first I would steal glances at a page or two; later I found myself reading whole chapters. Now I would consider no trip without a copy. When I read one of these volumes, I want to leap from my couch, strap on a backpack, throw away (or perhaps just hide) my credit cards, and travel cheaply to all of these wonderful and charming places. Of course the feeling soon passes; I regain my senses; and I check my wallet for the reassuring sight of a credit card. I highly recommend purchasing *Let's Go: Great Britain and Ireland* (New York: St. Martin's Press, annual). I have seen no other guide that contains so much information on train

/bus schedules, tourist offices, places to change money, laundromats, restaurants, and much more.

For fascinating overviews of the history of England, Scotland, and London as they relate to the modern traveller, I strongly recommend Interlink Publishing's *A Traveller's History of England*, *A Traveller's History of Scotland*, and *A Traveller's History of London*. Each volume in this series offers a complete and authoritative history from the earliest times up to the present day. A gazetteer cross-referenced to the main text pinpoints the historical importance of many of the sights and towns you will encounter on your walks.

Until I read Colin Fletcher's *Complete Walker*, my few desultory attempts at backpacking and wilderness walking were singularly unsuccessful. This book changed my walking life and made me a successful outdoorsperson. Even if you are only contemplating a walk through a city park, you will probably find some useful tips. Every conceivable topic is exhaustively treated. Wonderfully written in idiosyncratic "old codger" prose, the *Complete Walker III* (New York: Alfred A. Knopf, 1986) should be found in every walker's bookcase.

If you are anxious to order any of the optional maps and guides recommended below (see pp. 48–49) prior to arrival in Great Britain, telephone the bookstore Edward Stanford Ltd. at (0171) 836–1321. The staff is quite knowledgeable and they stock a vast selection of maps and guides. When in London, visit this excellent bookstore at 12–14 Longacre.

Level of Fitness

If you are already a regular walker, you should have no problem with any of the walks listed in this book. None of the walks require any serious climbing, but a few involve a number of breathtaking ups and downs. In the trail notes, I have listed the approximate amount of climbing that you will do on each trail. If you are not a frequent walker and not involved in an exercise program, you should begin walking regularly a couple of months before you arrive in Great Britain. The walks that I have included vary from about two to nine miles, with most ranging from three to six miles. If you can walk four to five miles before you leave, you should be able to complete all of the walks I have listed. There are a number of books that show you how to develop a walking-fitness program. I have never been able to read more than a few pages of such books and find it odd that so much ink has been devoted to such a simple and natural motion. I just begin with a few three-to-five-mile walks and increase the distance until I reach the maximum length of walk that I anticipate completing. At this level of walking fitness, I adjust quickly to walking in Great Britain.

Car Rental

If you have decided to drive, you should reserve a car before you leave for Great Britain. Renting a car once you have arrived is substantially more expensive. I always find the cheapest and most fuel-efficient vehicle. For up to three people who are not large and do not bring much luggage, the smallest vehicles are sufficient. It is best to comparison shop for rates, but I have always found Kemwel to be the least expensive on a long-term basis. The longer you use the car the better the price, and if you lease for a minimum of three weeks you will be able to secure good terms. You can order Kemwel's brochures at 1–800–678–0678. Ask for both the car-rental and car-lease brochures.

When to Go

Most people will go during the summer, but Great Britain's moderate climate allows for walking throughout the entire year. This does not mean that you will necessarily enjoy a walk through the Scottish Highlands in January, but, particularly in the south, many trails will be easily accessible throughout the entire year.

What to Bring

Money

With the less-than-impressive dollar hovering around £0.66, I budget about $75 per day if I am travelling alone. I find that an extra person adds about $35 to the expenses, adding up to about $110 per day.

I usually carry about $400 dollars worth of pounds in cash, and the rest in travellers checks also in British pounds. Travellers checks, in British pounds, are accepted at many hotels and some restaurants. However, since most proprietors seem to prefer cash or credit cards, I usually change travellers checks at a bank and pay cash for most transactions. Some banks charge a high commission for changing travellers' checks. Often the policy on commission will be posted. If it is not posted, avoid problems by asking before the transaction takes place. Visa and Mastercard are almost universally accepted.

Luggage

I bring one backpack which serves as check-in luggage. It carries almost everything except books, guides, maps, and other expensive items. You may wish to purchase a pack that has a disappearing suspension system as an alternative to a wilderness pack. Ordinary luggage with only a handle looks pathetically useless to me and, unless you have porters or are on a guided tour, it should be shunned.

I use what will be my hiking daypack as carry-on luggage. I own a Lowe Klettersack which is incredibly durable, comfortable, and capacious. I will discuss the use and selection of a daypack below. My third piece is a small shoulder bag that contains photographic equipment, mini cassette recorder, and a few other small items. When I arrive at the airport or park my car, I put the large pack on my back, strap the camera bag around my neck, hold the daypack with both arms, and stagger to my destination. I avoid bringing more than I can carry in one trip.

Clothing

Including what I am wearing on the plane, I bring four shirts, three pairs of pants, one pair of shorts, two pairs of regular socks, three pairs of wool hiking socks, four pairs of underpants, one hat, one sweater, one lightweight jacket, one pair of hiking boots, and one pair of walking shoes. Everything is color coordinated and can be easily washed and dried. Although I become quickly tired of these clothes, they are sufficient for months of touring and can be easily burned upon return from Great Britain.

Personal/Health Items

Always bring soap, since some lodgings do not feel obligated to assure that their clients are sparkling clean. I also bring multiple vitamins, which I usually forget to take, razors, scissors, dental floss, thick dental tape which I use to remove trapped, broken dental floss from between my teeth, toothbrush/paste, bandages for possible sprains, aspirin or aspirin substitute, bandaids, and toilet paper (which is not available at all British toilets). I do not bother with shampoo or conditioner, but you may have more hair and find bar-soap to be an inadequate hair cleanser.

Miscellaneous

Sewing needles and thick thread are useful for torn clothes, lost buttons, and damaged equipment. I always bring a high-quality small flashlight that runs on AA batteries to fend off uninvited darkness. An extra, easily-compressed small backpack is convenient for shopping around town and carrying laundry. I also carry a small towel which I have not yet employed for any task; however, I fear excluding it from my pack because I suspect that it will, at an unspecified future date, rescue me from some acute emergency situation. A small am-fm radio may break the silence of a televisionless B&B room. A lightweight electronic alarm will prod you from bed and ensure promptness to important transportation occurrences. I never go on any trip, foreign or domestic, without a lightweight goosedown sleeping bag. I have a North Face Light Rider, which weighs about two pounds and compresses to almost invisibility. A sleeping bag makes an excellent extra blanket and is indispensable when unrolled in its large storage sack as an extra large pillow that can allow you to sit comfortably upright on a bed with your head against the wall or headboard.

Daypack

On day hikes, I carry a Lowe Klettersac which, as I have mentioned, is strong and durable. It has a top pocket and is also large enough to carry the numerous items listed below. The Klettersac also has a narrow waistbelt that distributes some of the weight from my shoulders to my hips. The waistbelt also prevents the pack from shifting at some critical juncture where I might be sent hurtling into an uninviting abyss. Even if you are not carrying much weight, be certain to purchase a pack with well-padded straps and a waistbelt.

I am not able to enjoy a simple walk without a vast catalogue of items that are designed to ward off any and every conceivable problem. I envy the occasional person I see strolling down a remote trail wearing a disintegrating pair of sandals and carrying nothing more than a leaking bottle of mineral water. I have never had the spiritual levity that allows these people to face possible disaster or even discomfort with such nonchalance.

The items you select from the following list for your daypack will depend upon where you fall on the nonchalance/paranoia continuum. I will discuss my rationale for carrying and frequency of use for each item.

The most important item in or on your daypack is water. I prefer the taste of water that is carried in clear, unbreakable lexan bottles with a loop top that prevents the tragedy of lost bottle caps. I use the one-liter size that can be inserted into nylon bottle-holders. The bottle-holders have a velcro loop that can be placed over belts, and I loop one around an adjustment strap on the side of my pack. Depending on the length of the walk, I also carry one or two extra bottles in the pack where they stay cooler. Do not pick up a bottle of mineral water, throw it in your pack, and assume that you have a safe supply of water. Once, having lost a canteen the day before, I placed a bottle of mineral water in my wife's pack. After climbing twenty-five minutes directly uphill in cloudless heat, we threw down our packs. The sound of breaking plastic and flowing water has never been so grim. About 40% of our water supply for that day soaked the contents of my wife's pack. I do not remember the exact outcome, but we probably barely survived while trading ill-natured and acrimonious accusations. Had we gotten lost, our bones could still be blanching somewhere in Europe. Use only indestructible water containers, and do not lose them.

Powdered water additives such as Gatorade can be purchased in many larger supermarkets. They strike me as being expensive, but on longer, electrolyte-unbalancing walks I occasionally use them. They are also useful if you become weary of the taste of plain warm water.

On most walks, you will carry food. I usually bring some type of whole-grain bread, and I always have a supply of emergency *gauffrettes*. *Gauffrettes* are the chocolate or vanilla wafers that cause me to gain several pounds during a summer of walking. Most people have more sophisticated culinary desires and will be pleased with the variety of foods available even in smaller stores. For me, picnics involve too much organizing and general psychological stress. However, I realize that not everyone is going to find happiness sitting on a rock while gnawing on a loaf of bread.

I suspect that the concept of ozone depletion is actually a massive conspiracy by the world's sunscreen manufacturers; but, like an atheist who prays occasionally at bedtime, I am not sure and prepare for all possible outcomes. I do not like the slippery feel of sunscreen, and I still cannot bring myself to smear it on my balding, some say bald, head. However, I usually remember to put it on my face and arms. The best I have found is Coppertone's

Sport SPF 30, which clings tenaciously to my skin rather than dripping into my eyes. However, if the price escalates from the present seven dollars for four ounces, only the wealthiest of walkers will be able to afford its protection. Purchase sunscreen before you leave; in Great Britain it is even more expensive.

Although I seldom have blisters, I always include a package of Dr. Scholl's Moleskin in my daypack. Moleskin and similar products attach to skin in order to prevent sensitive spots from becoming blisters through frequent rubbing against a boot. I have used Moleskin on several occasions, and it has saved me from some painful miles. I also carry a small pair of scissors to properly shape the Moleskin.

As I mentioned before, toilet paper should always be kept within arms' reach. There are few toilets on trails and even fewer with toilet paper. Since toilets and reading material are frequently associated items, I should mention that I always bring a book, magazine, or newspaper on a walk. You may be trapped in a situation where you must wait for public transportation, or you may find an alluring spot that begs you to peruse that *Time* magazine whose covers you have been dying to get between.

I have lightweight binoculars that usually stay in my pack. Although they are seldom used, they can be valuable on less-frequently-marked trails that cross many treeless, rockless open fields. Binoculars enable you to scan distant rocks and trees for waymarks.

A mini-cassette recorder can be useful for recording thoughts and experiences while on the trail. I also use it to record trail sounds such as singing birds, quick moving rivers, and occasional conversations.

Although I counsel that you should always pack a poncho or other rain protection, I frequently leave it behind on sunny days. Of course, weather can change quickly in Great Britain and, proving my inability to learn from experience, I have been deeply saturated on several poncholess walks. In cooler weather, I also bring a nylon jacket, which I seldom use.

A map pouch that you can suspend from your body is also

indispensable. Silva, and other companies, make a variety of these pouches which should be waterproof and fasten with velcro tabs. They keep your maps and guides visible but dry and also store a variety of other small items.

Trail Garb: Not GQ

I usually wear lightweight cotton pants and shirts. I seldom wear shorts, but then neither do Arabs in the burning desert. In addition to blocking harmful UV rays, pants offer protection from dense, thorny overgrown trails and the clinging insects they harbor. Although all of the trails in this book are in good condition, it is not uncommon for uncovered legs to suffer abrasive attacks on some segments.

Since jogging or walking shoes do not offer tender soles enough protection from the frequently rocky trails, hiking boots always adorn my valuable feet. Also, because of rain and intersecting streams, trails will be frequently muddy. If you wear walking or jogging shoes on a damp trail, they will become quickly inundated. I own two pairs of Vasque Sundowners which currently retail for about $150 (£100). They are leather with a waterproof Gore-Tex lining and do not weigh heavily on my feet. They are the most comfortable boots that I have owned, but the soles seem to last only one summer. They can be resoled for about $50 (£35). If you do not currently own hiking boots, I suggest that you try several pairs before making a final decision.

I have both cotton and wool hiking socks. Both are comfortable, but I almost always wear the wool socks. I have no scientific explanation for this choice. I also have a hat which, unless it is raining, is found in my pack. A poncho and a nylon jacket, which I have already mentioned, complete my walking wardrobe.

2. When You Get There

Where to Stay

Since this book is designed for travellers at all budget levels, no specific lodging suggestions have been listed. However, lodgings in Great Britain are easy to book through the local tourist offices. They have listings at all levels of expense and can, usually for free, book your lodgings on the spot. I have never had any complaints about accomodations booked through tourist offices. All of the areas in this book have a tourist office, and most are easy to find via road signs within the city.

Food Consumption

Britain is not known for gourmet food, but there are many excellent restaurants catering to a variety of tastes. Standard meat/ fish, peas, and potatoes fare is available everywhere, but Great Britain has also become vegetarian-friendly with most restaurants offering a variety of non-meat entrées. Outside of London and other big cities, there are not many ethnic restaurants except the ubiquitous and usually excellent Indian restaurants. Less expensive meals can be had at local fish and chips establishments and also at pubs, where the quality of food has improved dramatically in recent years.

Public Transportation

All of these linear walks have been designed so that you will have the opportunity to be involved in short trips on public transportation, which introduces you into the life of small-town Britain. On rural buses, in particular, you will often believe that you have entered the driver's living room as he is entertaining guests. The regulars converse among themselves and the driver passes along the latest gossip, and it is not uncommon for an American visitor to be drawn into the discussion. Buses, unlike trains, however, are not always on time. Although they almost always appear, you should wait at least 30–40 minutes before abandoning hope. Complete instructions for local transportation are included in the trail notes in Part Two.

Driving

Even though escape from cars and traffic is one of the goals of a walking vacation, there is no inconsistency in writing about driving in a walking book. Ironically, your car will enable you to more efficiently avoid other cars and also give you the freedom to set your own schedule. You will be free from crowded long-distance public transportation and able to reach places that are not served by public transportation. Although there are some negatives, including expense, heavy traffic, difficult parking in large cities, and poorly marked roads, I would not enjoy Great Britain as much without the freedom a car allows.

3. Trail Life

Waymarking

In England the official long distance trails are waymarked with the sign of an acorn; in Scotland with a thistle. On other trails signposts often indicate the way with an arrow or other symbol. Generally, waymarking is quite good; however, any problems that arise from poor waymarking are noted in the trail notes for each walk.

Use of Trail Notes and Optional Maps

Great Britain has one of the finest systems of national cartography in the world. The Ordnance Survey (government surveying and map publishing agency) has mapped the entire nation in a variety of scales, and I have recommended two types for each walk. The most detailed 1:25,000 scale ($2\frac{1}{2}$ inches = one mile) Pathfinder maps show virtually every topographical detail and include public rights of way. Outdoor Leisure maps are in the same scale but usually include a larger area in a region of great natural beauty. These maps are highly recommended for anyone planning to expand their walking activities beyond the walks detailed in this book. Also recommended are the 1:50,000 scale ($1\frac{1}{4}$ inches = 1 mile) Landranger maps which show most public rights of way. They are adequate for well-trodden trails and also for general touring purposes.

Both of these maps are topographical, meaning they use what are called "contour lines" to give a detailed picture of how the land is shaped. If you know how to read a topographical map, you will be able to visualize where, how often, and how steeply you must climb on each walk. You will also be able to locate natural features such as lakes and rivers and man-made objects such as buildings and utility wires.

You should also purchase a compass with a transparent, rectangular base plate that can be used in conjunction with a topographical map. They are inexpensive and can always indicate in what direction you are travelling. If you follow the trail notes in this book, you will not need a compass. However, if you experiment with other trails or absentmindedly wander off the trails described in this book, there is always the possibility of becoming lost. Knowing how to use a map and compass has helped me stay found on a number of occasions. There are a number of books that offer instruction in the use of maps and compass. *Staying Found* by June Fleming (New York: Vintage, 1982) is clearly written and will teach you more than you ever wished to know about staying found.

If you do not learn from books, try orienteering. This is a rapidly growing international competitive sport. You are given a map and are required to find your way as quickly as possible through varied terrain. Along the way you must record certain codes that will prove that you have touched all points on a required route. There are several levels of competition, and novices are welcome. For more information, contact the United States Orienteering Federation, P.O. Box 1444, Forest Park, GA 30051.

How Often/How Far

I have included walks that are anywhere from two to nine miles with most in the four-to-six-mile range. Even if you only embark on an occasional short walk, you will experience Great Britain as have few other tourists.

Do not become obsessed with distance. This is not a competitive sport, and there is no point in consuming entire days with walking. You are on vacation and should enjoy not only the walks but the destinations. A four-to-six-mile walk will take you into the countryside and onto local public transportation for several hours. You will also get enough exercise to justify a calorie-laden dinner and will be tired enough to sleep well at night. Also re-member that you will often be walking several miles around tourist sites and your home base during the evening. A day in which you complete a six-mile walk can easily add up to a ten-mile walking day with such incidental walking.

Time of Day

In less travelled areas, you will occasionally have to arrange your walking schedule around available transportation. However, many areas have excellent public transportation and you can often ar-range the walks to fit your general schedule.

When I have a choice, I usually stagger onto the trail at about ten or eleven a.m. This is in contrast to conventional wisdom, which counsels early rising in order to beat the midday heat. Since I am never in any hurry to rise early and rush to any destination, I spend many days walking in the noon-day sun with only the occasional mad dog or Englishman as a companion.

Potential Problems

Great Britain's trails are almost always havens of tranquility with nothing to fear but fear itself. The walker is a familiar sight in Great Britain and his or her right to walk unmolested through the country-side is universally respected. You may trek without trepidation.

The Car: Where to Leave It

I prefer to leave the car at my final destination and take the bus or train back to my walk's starting point. This procedure assures me that my car, barring theft, will be there to transport me to my hotel when I have completed a walk. Also, I agonize over prob-lems that might arise with public transportation: a misread or obsolete schedule, a strike, acts of a supreme deity, etc. If you do not cherish the thought of being marooned at walk's end, leave your car at your destination.

Part Two
35 Great Walks

How to Use the Thirty-Five Walk Descriptions

Each walk listed below is organized into the following information:

1. **Key to Symbols**: One or more of the following symbols will be found in the box at the beginning of each walk description to give you an idea of what to expect to see on the way:

| Art/Museum | Abbey/Cathedral | Château | Castle | River | Forest |

| Cliffs | Mountains | Pre-Historic Site | Historic Town Center | Coast/Beach |

2. The **General Description**, which is a short compendium of the topography and historical sites that you will encounter along the route. No attempt has been made to be comprehensive, and it is suggested that you consult the guidebooks mentioned above and other sources for more comprehensive historical information.

3. The **Optional Maps** section provides you with maps that may make your walking experience more interesting, especially if you enjoy working with a topographical map or desire to expand your walking adventures in a particular area. Maps can be purchased almost anywhere when you arrive in Great Britain, and most guides will be available at bookstores in the general area of the walk described.

4. The **Time/Distance** section includes the length of time necessary to complete the walk at a rate of about $2\frac{1}{2}$–3 miles (4–5 km) per hour and the distance in miles and kilometers.

5. The location of **Toilet Facilities** along the trail has been included. Often, however, there are none, which is why information has also been included on the amount of privacy. In general, men should have little trouble relieving themselves anywhere along the trail. On trails where much privacy has been indicated, women should also have no problems. Even where a trail is noted as having little privacy, women will usually have a number of suitable opportunities. Also, remember that you can usually use toilets at pubs, restaurants, and train stations.

6. Where you can obtain **Refreshments**, either at a restaurant or pub, has also been noted. However, do not neglect to bring water with you on any walk.

7. Instructions on how to arrive at the starting point via automobile and public transportation have been included in the **Getting There** section.

8. The **Trail Notes** correspond to the map, and indicate the general course of the trail. They have been structured so that they may be marked with a check after corresponding landmarks have been achieved. Although the inclusion of a note does not necessarily indicate a problem, notes have been provided wherever problems exist. In any case, always watch for waymarks and study your map.

9. At the end of each section, some **Suggestions for More Walking** have been included. Wherever possible, other day walks have been included, as well as possibilities for shortening or extending each of the thirty-five selected walks.

Walk 1: Cambridge

Walk: **Kingston to Cambridge via the Wimpole Way**

160 mins.
8 miles (12.8 km)

General Description

The brisk thirty-minute bus ride to Kingston wanders along winding roads almost too narrow for the wide-bodied vehicle. Oncoming traffic appears to the passenger perilously close to a destructive encounter with the bus's nose. Perhaps this is why it seems that passenger entry/exit is optional at any moment. Note the startling admonition affixed to the left of the driver's seat: "Passengers entering or leaving the bus whilst it is in motion do so at their own risk." The truly adventurous will exit without the benefit of a halted bus, while the less confident will wait for the bus to pause. As the journey to Kingston continues, you will pass green forests, fertile fields, and traditional villages complacent in their comfortable prosperity.

Kingston, which marks the walk's beginning, was a renowned market town during the Middle Ages. What remains is an impressive ten-acre commons area that formerly accommodated vendors and entertainers of all types. To your right as you walk north from the commons you will pass a cobblestone twelfth-century church; take a three minute walk around this venerable structure and its requisite cemetery. A few minutes later you will arrive in Caldecote, which means "cold cottages"—a good name to give your village if you want to make it sound less appealing to winter marauders. Here you will pass another attractive church cemetery that is certainly worth a moment's pause.

As you continue the trail out of Caldecote you will walk along the Cambridgeshire and Isle of Ely Naturalist Trust Nature Reserve, a densely wooded area harboring numerous birds and other unseen creatures who rustle and slither in the foliage that parallels the trail. Someone travelling from Kingston or Caldecote to

Cambridge during the Middle Ages might have passed along these same tracks.

Habitation at Coton (Old English for "cottages") probably dates from the Anglo-Saxon invasions of the fifth or sixth century. This is an extremely placid village only about $2\frac{1}{2}$ miles (4 km) from Cambridge. By now you may be thirsty and ready for a refreshing beverage at one of the two pubs in town. There is also a small general store where you can purchase snacks. Eat greedily across the street on the park bench which has a plaque inscribed "In Memory of Arthur Melbourne-Cooper: A Pioneer of the British Film Industry Who Lived and Died in Coton November 24, 1961 at the Age of 88 Years." He would be proud; it is a very nice bench.

The final walk into Cambridge takes you through a rustic band of green behind the colleges called the Backs; across the River Cam with its gondola-like punts ferrying tourists; and finally among the stately university buildings.

In Cambridge's cacophonous student atmosphere, the drone of English is frequently punctuated by a multitude of foreign tongues. In the space of a few blocks you may hear German, Spanish, Italian, Japanese, and other unidentifiable sounds from numerous, exotic lands.

Cambridge University houses numerous architectural masterpieces dating back to its founding in the late thirteenth century. The colleges and other sights are too numerous to list here, but the tourist office bulges with helpful information. You may also note that Cambridge has a spacious appearance due to the large commons fields which are used for numerous athletic activities. Try not to step on the middle-aged men who litter the fields, displaying their pale corpulence as if exposed to the burning sun of the French Riviera.

In this walker-friendly but driver-hostile city, street signs seem to be optional and only occasionally placed in obscure locations at the discretion of charitable building owners. Without any clear way of identifying your location it is possible to drive lost and in despair of finding your hotel. Buy a good city map and pray.

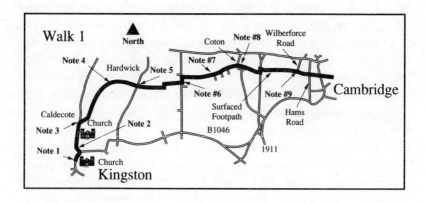

Optional Maps: Landranger 154/Pathfinder 1003; brochure "The Wimpole Way" available at the tourist office for £0.40

Time/Distance: 2 hours 40 minutes/8 miles (12.8 km)

Difficulties: Possible mud on rainy days; wear boots

Toilet Facilities: None, but much privacy until Coton

Refreshments: General store and two bars that serve food at Coton

Getting There: Buses run from Cambridge's Drummer Street to Kingston (#118) approximately every two hours. Bus schedules are available at the tourist office. If you are in a hurry, there is a taxi stand near the bus station.

Trail Notes

NOTE: The trail is not marked until after Caldecote, but there is no difficulty in following it. Bring your city map to guide you back to your car or hotel when you reach Cambridge.

___ 1a. The bus stops at the commons area of Kingston. If you prefer, the driver can stop at the church; however, this will save you only a few minutes of walking.

___ 1b. From either the commons or the church, walk directly north along the road that the bus entered the town.

___ 1c. As you pass the church look to your left; in the distance you will see another church at Caldecote which is your immediate destination.

___ 2. About five minutes beyond the first church, you will intersect with an asphalt road (B1046); turn left and then turn right a few minutes later onto another asphalt road which is marked with a sign indicating Caldecote.

___ 3. After you pass the church at Caldecote, begin looking to your right. In about five to six minutes, you will see a wooden sign "Public Bridleway, The Wimpole Way." Turn right here. (After you turn down this trail, you will begin to see wooden posts with blue arrows and a drawing of Wimpole Hall.)

___ 4. About forty minutes into the walk you will turn right into a field; the turn is clearly marked. You are now going in an easterly direction and will continue almost directly eastward until you reach Cambridge.

___ 5. When you reach a concrete road (55 minutes), turn left and then begin to watch to your right. You will see a Wimpole Way sign almost immediately that will direct you right.

___ 6. You will cross a second concrete road about twenty minutes later. Again, turn left and look right for the Wimpole Way signpost.

___ 7. After about ninety minutes you will merge with an asphalt road as you begin the walk into Coton.

___ 8a. Continuing down the same road, do not be tempted to turn right where you see a green "Public Footpath" sign that indicates a trail beyond a stone wall.

___ 8b. A few minutes beyond the church you will reach a dead end at an asphalt road. Turn right and continue along that same road as it veers left. You will soon see a pub called the Plough and a footpath sign indicating the Wimpole Way. You will take this footpath directly into Cambridge.

___ 9. You will begin your entry into Cambridge on Adams Road and will continue to the city center following the bike path signs.

Suggestions for More Walking

The Wimpole Way extends for only 13 miles from Wimpole Hall, the most spectacular eighteenth-century mansion and grounds in Cambridgeshire, to Cambridge. If you are in a hurry, take the bus or a cab to Coton and walk the 2½ miles (4 km) back to Cambridge (begin with note 7). If you wish to add an extra six miles (9.6 km) to the walk, take the infrequent bus to Arrington where you may walk less than one mile to Wimpole Hall via the Harcamlow Way and join the Wimpole Way to Kingston and eventually back to Cambridge. Be certain to have the O.S. (Ordinance Survey) Pathfinder map 1003 and the Wimpole Way brochure which is available at the Cambridge tourist office. Another attractive seven-mile (11.2 km) walk will take you along the River Cam from the town of Waterbeach to Cambridge. This towpath, known as the Haling Way, is clearly visible on both Pathfinder (982) and Landranger (154) maps.

Walk 2: York

Walk: Strensall to York via the Ebor Way

General Description

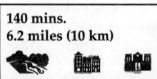

140 mins.
6.2 miles (10 km)

Do this walk before visiting the city and experience York as a medieval traveller—passing through an imposing gate, scurrying along narrow shop-filled streets, and being stunned by the enormity of the city's great cathedral.

Although rapidly becoming a bedroom community for York, Strensall does harbor a fine church and a small old quarter. You will not tarry long in town, however, before crossing the oxymoronic, vintage-1798 New Bridge where you will join the trail. This single-lane, almost two-centuries-old bridge remains uncrumbled and still bears vehicular traffic—a monument to proper spending of taxpayers' money, since it cost only about £1300 to build (what some London hotels expropriate for a luxury-class suite).

The River Foss, which parallels the trail for most of the walk, slinks slowly and shallowly along its winsome course, occasionally choked with emerald-colored vegetation, singing its swan song and perhaps remembering its thundering youth. The river and trail follow an engaging course through golden grain fields embellished with brilliant red poppy flowers, pastures where sheep and cows manage to live in peaceful coexistence with new construction, and encroaching suburbs (doesn't sound too romantic, but how many American tourists have the opportunity to walk through an English suburb—a learning experience not found on any other type of tour!). As you approach York, well-mannered water lilies, worthy of a Monet canvas, float languorously along the Foss. An occasional frog bellows and birds chirp and warble as you approach the city gates in a park-like atmosphere. Along the way, you will also see some curiosities, such as a fence constructed out of nineteenth-century rail cars by some practical-minded train fanatic and the very British sign that soberly states "Power Cables: Headroom 16 feet" (taller walkers beware!). What stands as most remarkable is the possibility of taking what is a mostly rural track directly into the heart of a modern metropolis—a back door open only to walkers.

York is protected by a circuit of well-scrubbed and well-maintained medieval walls which are occasionally used by locals to pour large vats of boiling oil onto hordes of invading tourists. Actually York, which stands gracefully at the confluence of the rivers Ouse and Foss, easily accommodates the crowds. Its origins can be traced to 71 AD when it was founded as a Roman fortress. Constantine, of legalizing-Christianity-fame, was proclaimed emperor here in 306. Later ruled by Vikings and Normans, York eventually assumed the role of England's second city. Today it is a lively tourist center and home to Britain's largest Gothic cathedral (250 years to complete). Walkers will want to take the $2\frac{1}{2}$ mile (4 km) walk around the ramparts which serves as an excellent introduction to the city. The Yorkshire Museum, which harbors the remains of St. Mary's Abbey on its grounds, is also worth a visit, as is the National Railway Museum, home of brilliantly restored steam locomotives.

Optional Maps: Landranger 100, 105/Pathfinder 655, 665

Time/Distance: 2 hours 20 minutes/6.2 miles (10 km)

Difficulties: Possible overgrown path for the first thirty minutes (see trail notes)

Toilet Facilities: None, but some privacy until Haxby

Refreshments: None until York

Getting There: Bus #3, #3B, or #X3 from York to Strensall—bus information is available next to the tourist office, and buses run quite regularly. Be certain that the bus you board is going to Strensall. Ask the bus driver to drop you off at York Road and Middlecroft Drive and point you in the direction of the New Bridge.

Trail Notes

NOTE: It is best to bring a city map to help guide you back to your car or hotel. However, everyone speaks English and you will not become lost without one.

___ 1a. When you exit the bus in Strensall, continue to walk north up York Road, the road you arrived on.

___ 1b. You will turn left where you see the chevronned traffic sign onto a street called West End.

___ 1c. In about 4–5 minutes, you will pass an elementary school. Turn right just beyond the school where you see a sign indicating "Haxby $2\frac{1}{2}$ miles."

___ 1d. You will turn right on a road called "West Pit Lane/Lead-

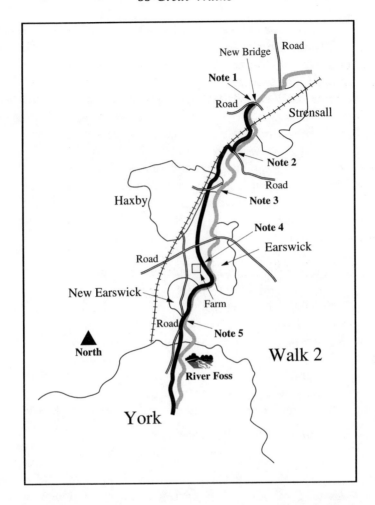

ing to Riverside Walk" and then walk over a narrow asphalt bridge called the New Bridge.

___ 1e. Turn left just over the bridge where a sign indicates "Public Footpath." (Important: If the path is heavily overgrown with vegetation, walk on the other side of the river which is usually well groomed and takes you to the same destination.)

___ 2. After about thirty minutes of following the river, you will come to a traffic bridge (you have already passed beneath a train bridge). Ascend to the two-lane asphalt road and turn right. Follow this road as it makes a sharp left turn. (You will soon see a sign to your left that indicates "Footpath: Centenary Way." Ignore it; it will just take you back to the bridge.)

___ 3. Shortly after you enter Haxby (there is a sign), the road you are on will turn sharply right. You, however, will continue straight ahead on a narrow concrete path (soon to be dirt), which is marked by a footpath sign.

___ 4. Shortly after you carefully cross a major road, you will come to a farm that is gated shut (about 1 hour 10 minutes). Turn left here along the fence and you will soon reach the River Foss, where you will turn right and rejoin the river.

___ 5a. You will be obliged to walk along a busy thoroughfare (1 hour 40 minutes into the walk) for a few minutes but this presents no problem since there is a sidewalk. Continue to look left; you will see signs indicating the Ebor Way and the Foss Walk that will bring you back to the river.

___ 5b. Continue along the river, now within York, until you reach the junction of Huntington (which follows the river) and Monkgate Roads. Turn right onto Monkgate Road and you will soon enter the walls of York through the Monk Gate.

Suggestions for More Walking

The Ebor Way rolls through Yorkshire for about seventy miles (112 km). See Ken Piggin's *The Ebor Way: A 70-Mile Walk from Helmsley to Ilkley through the Ancient City of York*, Northern Leisure Publications, 1990. For a short, pleasant walk (3 miles/4.8 km), take the bus to Bishopthorpe, visit the thirteenth-century Archbishop of York's palace and walk back to York along the River Ouse. For a longer walk (12 miles/19.3 km), take the bus to Tadcaster where you will join a Roman road through Copmanthorpe and into Bishopthorpe and then York.

Walk 3: Medieval Past

Walk: **Ripon to Fountains Abbey**

General Description

110 mins.
5 miles (8 km)

Ripon is a thriving town built around a teeming two-acre market place. Not a town to forget its medieval heritage (or perhaps still frightened by marauders from the surrounding forests), the citizens of Ripon employ a man to sound the horn at 9 p.m. every night to signal the beginning of the night watch. Ripon is also one of England's smallest cathedral towns and a visit to the twelfth-century cathedral will hold you momentarily from the trail, as will many intriguing shopping opportunities in the central town.

As you enter the trail from Ripon you will pass through grain fields adorned by numerous wild flowers and soon enter Studley Roger, a well-kept, one-street hamlet with a few shops. Ascending from Studley Roger, glance over your shoulder for excellent views of Ripon and the surrounding valley. From this point, a well-timbered, riverside path will guide you to the extensive grounds of Studley Royal and Fountains Abbey. Created in the eighteenth century by a disgraced but not impoverished Chancellor of the Exchequer, these water gardens are considered to be the most spectacular in all of England. Prodigious efforts were required for the completion of the gardens: the course of the River Skell was changed to give it a central location in the valley, artificial ponds were situated at aesthetically pleasing locations, and a conically shaped mound was installed on the formerly level ground. In spite of their artificial heritage, the grounds remain untamed in appearance and retain a sense of romantic savageness. The seven stone bridges that span the meandering river have a charm found nowhere else in England, and lovely Studley Lake, which the trail circumambulates, is inhabited by some of the most domesticated geese in England. Do not extend your hand unless you have something to feed them.

Enormous and mysterious, the splendid ruins of Fountains Abbey are second to none in evoking a feeling of times and lives long since past. Begun in the twelfth century and occupied over the next several centuries, the abbey eventually became unproductive and fell into ruin. In 1768, William Aislabie, owner of neighboring Studley Royal, purchased the abbey as an ornamental addition to his extensive gardens. The extensive ruins are the most complete in England and were once the center of a thriving agricultural and industrial community. If they would fit, I would like them in my back yard. This is a suitable place to relax and reflect on time's passage.

Optional Maps: Landranger 99/Pathfinder 653; a free (but not always accurate) map "A Walk from Ripon to Studley Royal" available at Ripon tourist office

Time/Distance: 1 hour 50 minutes/5 miles (8 km)

Difficulties: Some minor climbs

Toilet Facilities: None between end points, but some privacy

Refreshments: None en route

Getting There: By car: From York, drive west via A59 to Harrogate where you will switch to A61 north. At Ripon go west on B6265. Continue past the main park entrance and take the first road to the left which leads to the old entrance, a car park, and the bus stop. Buses run early on every school day (about 8:30 a.m.), but only on Thursday and Sunday from late July to September. Call United at Darlington 468771, or take the short ride by taxi and do the walk in reverse. *By Public Transportation*: Several United buses per day run between Ripon and York. Once in York, you can opt to begin the walk in Ripon or Fountains Abbey, whichever best fits the bus schedules.

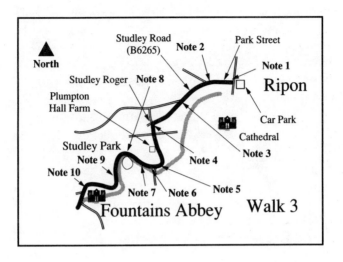

Trail Notes

___ 1. From Ripon's Market Square, the town center, walk out of town via Park Street which becomes Studley Road (B6265).

___ 2. Be certain to bear left at the first fork just past the tennis courts; do not go directly ahead onto Clotherholme Road.

___ 3. After you cross a bridge, begin to look left. About 3–4 minutes later you will see a public footpath sign indicating "Studley Roger." (Do not take the path to the right which is about 100 feet before the one you are looking for and indicates "Public Footpath/Galphay Lane.")

___ 4. When you reach Studley Roger's only through street, turn left and continue down the asphalt road passing the impressive gate to Studley Royal and Plumpton Hall Farm.

___ 5. Soon after you pass Plumpton Hall Farm, you will turn right onto a deeply wooded dirt trail.

___ 6. When you come to the first fork on this trail, there are no waymarks to help you find your way. Bear right; do not go left over a dried riverbed. (If you are using the map from the tourist office at Ripon, it fails you by indicating a crossing of the river at this point. It continues to be useless until you reach Studley Lake.)

___ 7. Soon, when you have passed through a wooden gate, you will be on the grounds of Fountains Abbey. Simply follow the river and cross the always-visible stone bridges.

___ 8. When you get to the small lake, cross the wooden foot-bridge and continue on the path around the lake.

___ 9. As you finish the walk around the lake you will reach the tourist office where you must pay the £3.80 admission charge. Also pick up a copy of the park map. Just continue along the asphalt path to the abbey.

___ 10. Continue down the same path that led to the abbey; it will take you out of the park. Turn left as you exit and you will soon see the car park and bus stop.

Suggestions for More Walking

Unfortunately, this beautiful area is poorly served by public transportation, and trails are not well marked. However, one possibility for a short walk is to take the bus to Bishop Monkton from Ripon and walk the 3½ miles (5.6 km) back along trails and country lanes through Littlethorpe to Ripon.

Walk 4: North Sea

Walk: Scarborough to Filey via the Cleveland Way

General Description

180 mins.
8 miles (12.8 km)

Scarborough grew slowly from a medieval village into a twentieth-century resort. The catalyst for growth was the seventeenth-century discovery of a spring whose waters were reputed to cure most maladies, including a form of hypochondria. Today, well-preserved Scarborough Castle is the focus of local tourist activity. Constructed during the twelfth century, the castle, in its enormity, covers eleven acres and also houses the remains of a Roman signal station. You can walk or drive to the castle's precipitous perch for a close inspection of the walls and other structures. The castle separates the town's two beaches, which on a sunny day form havens for stout working- and middle-class Britons. Before you begin your ramble, take a moment to stroll the medieval streets south of the castle and wander about the old fishing harbor. Departing Scarborough, many charming homes constructed at the turn of the century for a prosperous middle class will line your path.

The way to Filey is a remarkable cliff-top and beach trek with omnipresent views of the North Sea. Glimpses of Scarborough and its imposing fortress are also present throughout much of the walk. Watch for the frequent concrete bunkers designed to protect Britain from Nazi invasion that dot the beach at deadly intervals and still defend the British from invasion by continental rabble.

Like Scarborough, Filey is a working-class resort. If an Englishman cannot afford the south of France, the North Sea will have to do. However, in contrast to occasionally stately Scarborough, Filey has the atmosphere of an itinerant carnival that has lost its mobility. Here, England is at its least elegant—muscle shirts and tattoos are everywhere and on both sexes.

Optional Maps: Landranger 101/Pathfinder 624

Time/Distance: 3 hours/8 miles (12.8 km)

Difficulties: The trail can be occasionally overgrown; boots and long pants are advised.

Toilet Facilities: Scarborough, Filey, and about midway near the café

Refreshments: At the café about midway

Getting There: The A165 links Filey and Scarborough if you are driving. There are frequent trains and buses between the two towns.

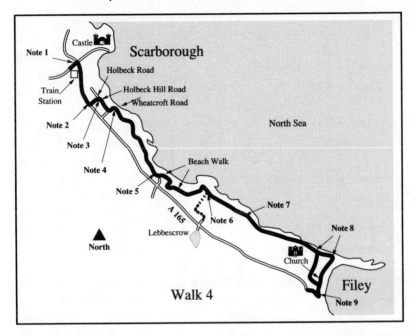

Trail Notes

Purchasing the city map, at either town's tourist office, which covers both Filey and Scarborough, is a good idea.

___ 1. As you exit the train station in Scarborough, turn right and walk to the first street which is Westbrough, where you again turn right, walking in a southerly direction. (Do not worry about name changes, just continue down this commercial thoroughfare which after about 10 minutes becomes residential in nature.)

___ 2. Watch for Holbeck Road (about 18 minutes) where you will turn left and at the end of the road see the sea.

___ 3. When you get to the next street, Holbeck Hill Road, turn right. You will see a Cleveland Way sign.

___ 4. When you get to Wheatcroft Avenue, turn left. You will soon see a Cleveland Way sign that points you right.

___ 5. After about 1 hour 5 minutes, you will descend to the beach from the cliffs where you have been walking. Continue down the beach until you notice a small white building with a café sign. Go up the stairs here and continue south on the trail.

___ 6. Do not turn right on the path marked "Lebberston."

___ 7. When you reach the caravan park, continue straight ahead in front of the caravans. It will appear that you are walking through their front yards, but you are on the correct path and will soon see a trail sign.

___ 8. When you approach Filey, look to your right for a trail that leads to a church. You may turn right here and the trail will take you to the beach, or you may turn right at the next trail which also takes you to the beach at Filey.

___ 9. When you descend to the beach at Filey, you will be on Beach Street. Walk in a southerly direction and turn right where you see the sign "Cobol Landing"; this is Cargate Hill Road. As you ascend, the tourist office is to your left in the large house. This road leads to both the bus and train stations.

Suggestions for More Walking

Filey forms one end of the 110-mile semi-circular Cleveland Way, which skirts the North Sea cliffs for forty-five miles before turning west along a circuitous route within the North York Moors National Park. The most recent and authoritative guide is Ian Sampson's *Cleveland Way*, Aurum Press, 1990. The nine-mile walk from Scarborough to Ravenscar will take you into the park and along the cliffs but public transportation to Ravenscar is limited. A much longer eighteen-mile trek from Scarborough to Whitby can be done with the aid of very regular public transportation.

Walk 5: North York Moors

Walk: **Helmsley Castle to Rievaulx Abbey**

70 mins.
3 miles (4.8 km)

General Description

The 550-square-mile North York Moors National Park, one of England's largest remaining expanses of wilderness, lies about thirty miles north of York. However, it is not a wilderness in the American sense, for this area has been populated for many centuries and even today towns, castles, and abbeys punctuate the supernaturally beautiful forests, moors, and rugged coastline. Two of the park's finest sites, Rievaulx Abbey and Helmsley Castle, are linked by a provocatively picturesque and easy-to-follow trail.

Originally a sturdy Norman stronghold, now a casualty of time's inexorable advance, Helmsley Castle still looms ominously over its town. Constructed during the twelfth century, the castle keep, surrounded by massive earthworks, still stands at its original height. However, half of the keep was destroyed during the English Civil War, giving it a ghostly profile not to be missed on a foggy day. Helmsley, the town, is considered to be one of the most attractive settlements in Yorkshire and continues to shelter a marketplace that has thrived since Anglo-Saxon times. This pleasant, gray-stone town with excellent accommodations and shopping can also make a good base of operations for further exploration of the park and marks the beginning of the Cleveland Way, one of the major national trails.

The path commences along a shady country lane in the bucolic serenity of this rolling pasture and farmland. Even on an overcast day, an abundance of wild flowers illuminate your passage. Soon you will enter a densely forested area adorned with both coniferous and deciduous trees—a world of verdant luminosity which at times becomes as dense as a rainforest. As you approach the abbey, the full-flowing River Rye becomes your very pleasant companion, and grazing sheep dot the gentle slopes beyond the river.

First glimpsed, twelfth-century Rievaulx Abbey, abandoned in this lonely valley for hundreds of years, is a stunningly romantic sight. The ruins rise gracefully and, paradoxically, deathlessly from the pristine beauty of the Rye Valley. In addition to the impressive church, there are a variety of other ruins, including an infirmary, chapel, kitchens, and a warming house. It is not difficult to visualize monastic life while ambling through these striking relics of a lost world.

Optional Maps: Landranger 100/Outdoor Leisure Map North York Moors: Western Area #26

Time/Distance: 1 hour 10 minutes/3 miles (4.8 km) (there and back, 2 hours 20 minutes/6 miles or 9.6 km)

Difficulties: Some minor climbs

Toilet Facilities: At Helmsley and Rievaulx

Refreshments: None between sites

Getting There: From York, go north on B1363, which ends at B1257. Turn left on B1257, which leads to Helmsley. Buses run from York to Helmsley on Tuesday, Thursday, and Saturday. (Hutchinson Coaches—tel. Coxwold (01845) 401232 or inquire at York tourist office.) Buses between Rievaulx and Helmsley run only on Fridays and Sundays at mid-morning and mid-afternoon (tel. Stokesley 710324, or tourist office at Helmsley 01439-70173). Taxis can take you from Helmsley to Rievaulx, but they may be busy when you arrive at Helmsley so reserve ahead. If public transportation does not suit your schedule, the walk there and back is easy and pleasant.

Trail Notes

___ 1. The trail begins at the car park near the castle. You will see a sign indicating the Cleveland Way. The path is well marked and easy to follow from this point.

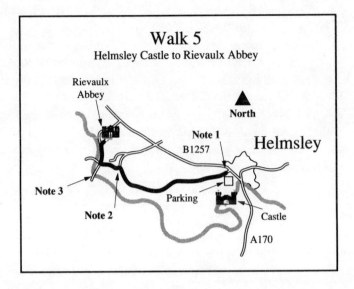

Walk 5
Helmsley Castle to Rievaulx Abbey

___ 2. When you arrive at an asphalt vehicular road, turn left. There will be a sign "Cleveland Way Rievaulx Abbey One Mile."

___ 3. When you come to the bridge over the River Rye, turn right. You will soon be at the abbey. (If you return on foot from the abbey just reverse the walk and be certain to join the dirt path at the correct spot, which is marked.)

Suggestions for More Walking

See the suggestions under Walk 4 for more information about the Cleveland Way. The Helmsley tourist office has a brochure "A Stroll Around Helmsley," which describes a one-hour walk through the town and immediate countryside. The four-mile round trip from Helmsley southwest to Harome along the River Rye via the Ebor Way and country lanes is pleasant and easy (clearly marked on O.S. Landranger 100). Numerous brochures and guides describing walks within the park are available at the park information centers in Helmsley, Sutton Bank, and Danby.

Walk 6: Roman Heritage: Hadrian's Wall

Walk: **Roman Military Museum to Once Brewed (National Park Information Center) via the Penine Way**

150 mins.
6.5 miles (10.5 km)

General Description

It was during Hadrian's reign that the boundaries of the Roman Empire were defined, gradually contracting but never expanding again. The northernmost boundary was set along a narrow band in what is now the north of England. In order to protect his empire from less-than-savory savages from the north, Hadrian had an eighty-mile (129 km) wall constructed along a hilly course from the North Sea to the Atlantic Ocean. Although not impregnable, the wall severely limited raids and full-scale invasions. Invaders realized that once over the wall, they would be soon met by Roman reinforcements and encircled since any retreat would be blocked by Roman soldiers manning the walls. The remains of the wall and the forts along its path are among England's finest sights, and the best way of experiencing this world heritage site is on foot. Often steep and rocky with winds robbing you of what little breath you have when you are ascending, the initial forty minutes of this walk will cure all but the most recalcitrant cases of insomnia. After this jagged trial, the trail becomes fairly level.

You must walk the wall to get a true understanding of its impressiveness. Tourists who are driven to a couple of sections to gape at the stones never understand the wall in pre-transportation-revolution human terms. The leisurely pace of foot transportation also allows for a savoring of unparalleled vistas—there are limitless horizons in all directions. Muse about the expense of constructing and defending such a wall in pre-modern times, and ponder the thesis that overextended military commitments result in the decline of great powers.

For the Romans, this was truly the end of the world, and their knowledge of what existed in the unknown beyond was based on rumor and speculation. What terror might have gripped the Romans as they peered warily over the wall at those bleak northern expanses? What awe might the barbarians have felt when they looked at this alien structure, a product of a civilization that was so far beyond their primitive technology? Wild tales and misconceptions must have circulated on both sides.

The wall trek will transport you far into the past, but even along remote stretches of the trail, the twentieth century occasionally intrudes. B&B signs directing the walker from the wall to some lonely farmhouse for rest and repast dot the rocky landscape, and military jets roar past in practice maneuvers, reminding the traveller how much the world has changed since the time of Hadrian. Finally, if you are wondering why the entire wall is not intact, look around at all the stone walls that divide the local fields.

Optional Maps: Landranger 86/Pathfinder 546

Time/Distance: 2 hours 30 minutes/6.5 miles (10.5 km)

Difficulties: Frequent climbs and descents, some quite steep; path often quite rocky

Toilet Facilities: About midway at a Crawfield's picnic site where there is a car park; some privacy at other points

Refreshments: None between end points

Getting There: From either Hexham or Carlisle, which are the area's two major tourist centers, drive via A69 to Henshaw, where you will see the signs directing you to Once Brewed and the National Park Information Center. From late July until early September, the Hadrian's Wall Bus Service runs along the length of the wall on B6318 between Hexham and Haltwhistle. There are four buses per day at two-hour intervals beginning around 10 a.m. except Sundays when service is reduced. Information about exact

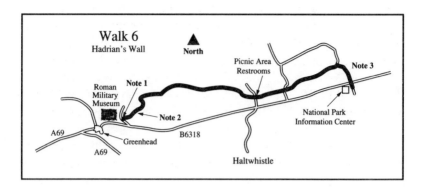

times can be obtained from the National Park Information Centre (tel. (01434–344396). From the Information Center, take the bus to the Roman Military Museum where the walk begins. If you arrive at a time before or after the period when buses are running, the staff at the Once Brewed information center can call a taxi to take you to the museum (about £5). However, it may be wise to reserve ahead.

Trail Notes

___ 1. After you visit the Roman Military Museum, you may ask the staff to direct you to the trail or simply walk straight ahead on the narrow asphalt road as you leave the museum grounds.

___ 2. As you walk down the narrow asphalt road, look to your left and about 50–75 yards down the road you will see a signpost indicating "Penine Way," which is the direction you should take. There should be no problem, but if you are confused, ask or follow other walkers. From this point, you should have no problem following the wall which seems to take in all of the highest points. When you cross fields, simply look for the ladders over the stone walls.

___ 3. After about 2 hours 15 minutes, you will come to an asphalt road. To your left, you will see the parking lot at Steel Rigg (the first parking lot since you departed from the picnic area where the restrooms are located); turn right here on the asphalt road which will lead you back to the National Park Information Center.

Suggestions for More Walking

The Penine Way is one of Britain's most venerable and rugged long-distance trails. This 256-mile (412 km) trek was the first and is still the most famous of Britain's official trails. There are numerous guides to this trail both complete and covering only certain segments. The most recent are Tony Hopkins' *Penine Way North* and *Penine Way South*, Aurum Press in association with the Countryside Commission and the Ordnance Survey, 1989. There are a variety of circular walks in the vicinity of the wall, and if public transportation does not fit into your schedule, try the circular walk "Steel Rigg, Hadrian's Wall," which is mapped with directions on a laminated card available at the information center (£0.50). Other short walks are possible and the information center staff are very helpful.

Walk 7: Edinburgh/Fife Coast

Walk: **Crail to Pittenweem via the Fife Coast Walk**

| 120 mins. |
| 5.5 miles (8.8 km) |

General Description

The city-weary will rejoice in this secluded stop on the way to the North. Weatherbeaten fishermen still ply their trade, and the villages still cater to local rather than tourist needs—there are no trendy facades or yuppie cafés. This fascinating walk will take you through three of the finest Fife-coast fishing villages and along much pristine coastal territory. At Crail, the trail head, there is a venerable stone harbor that still protects crab and lobster boats and a group of eighteenth-century buildings worthy of a roll of film. There is also a small sandy beach in Crail, but most of the coast is cluttered with large dark rocks, some quite jagged and menacing.

Departing Crail, you will notice, in the distance, ruins of Scotland's first lighthouse (1630) on the Isle of May. To your right you will see ruins of abandoned homes as you walk through herds of grazing cows who only grudgingly allow passage to the occasional walker.

Just outside of Anstruther you will pass the finest pig farm in Scotland. Pigs of all sizes range over numerous acres wallowing at will and then retiring when fatigued to pig-sized, wolf-proof quanset huts complete with straw at the entrance to wipe off their hoofs after a day's frolicking. I suspect that they would frolic less if they knew their ultimate destiny.

As you pass into Anstruther (Anstruther Easter and Wester are contiguous and usually referred to by the singular appellation "Anstruther") you will see one of the numerous homely caravan parks that scar many of Britain's most scenic areas providing million-dollar views for a negligible investment. Except for larcenous sea gulls roaming around town blatantly displaying purloined fish in their pointy mouths, Anstruther is a quiet, unassuming village where residents dry clothes along sturdy ropes in the scenic harbor. All sorts of commerce and an excellent tourist information office are found in town. There is also a Scottish Fisheries Museum and boat tours to the Isle of May, which is now a wildlife preserve. As you depart Anstruther next to a golf course, watch for a most eloquent do-not-defecate-here sign: "Notice hereby given that it is an offense to permit a dog to deposit excrement upon this place. Maximum fine £100." I saw no excrement on this portion of the trail. When you reach Pittenweem, stop for a quick beverage and enjoy the nautical atmosphere; this is the Fife Coast's busiest fishing port and a fine terminus for a unique walk.

Optional Maps: Landranger 59/Pathfinder 374

Time/Distance: 2 hours/5.5 miles (8.8 km)

Difficulties: None

Toilet Facilities: At all three villages

Refreshments: At all three villages

Getting There: From Edinburgh, take A90 over the Forth Road Bridge. After passing the bridge continue straight ahead on M90 until you reach A92. At Kirkcaldy you will continue east on A915 and then on A917, which enters Pittenweem. Park your car somewhere along the harbor area where you will be arriving on foot later. If you do not have a car, plan on spending the night at Pittenweem or elsewhere in the area. Buses run regularly along the Fife Coast but take about three hours to get from Edinburgh to Pittenweem (inquire at the Edinburgh tourist office for schedule information). If you are spending time in Edinburgh this will make an excellent overnight excursion. Walk up to the main road (A917) and ask anyone where the bus stops, which is in front of the Pittenweem Curiosity Shop. (In this small town everyone knows, and they will probably be able to tell you when the next bus leaves.) Buses to Crail (#95, but feel free to stop any bus to ask when the next one to Crail will arrive) run approximately every hour. You can also stop at the Leven tourist office to pick up a schedule on your way to Pittenweem or call the head office of Fife Scottish at Kirkcaldy (01592) 261461.

Trail Notes

___ 1a. From the bus stop at Crail, walk back towards Pittenweem on the main road. Look to your left; you will see a street with a hedge on one side called "Westbraes Street leading to Osborne Terrace." Walk down this street where you will see a public footpath sign.

___ 1b. Continue along this road in front of a row of stone town houses, pass through the gate, and you will be on the trail. From this point the trail is easy to follow and obvious. (Alternatively, and only rock climbers will enjoy this op-

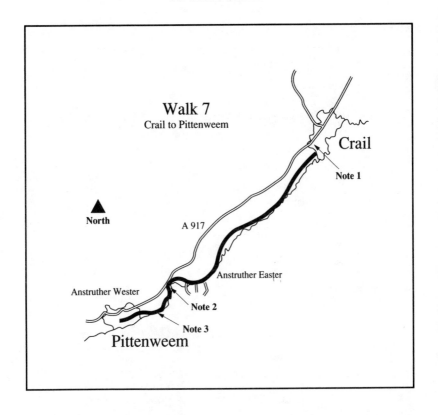

Walk 7
Crail to Pittenweem

Crail

Note 1

North

A 917

Anstruther Easter

Anstruther Wester

Note 2

Note 3

Pittenweem

tion, you can walk down to the harbor and inch forward precariously across the rocky coast until you are able to find a way up to the trail where the rocks meet the grass).

____ 2a. Through Anstruther, you will be walking along a shore road called Shore Street which becomes Castle Street.

____ 2b. When you get to the end of Castle Street, turn right. Then take a quick left onto the main road called High Street (A91).

____ 2c. You will continue for a short while along High Street until you reach Crichton Street and turn left; then turn right at the first street (Shore Road), which leads you back to the trail.

____ 3. At the golf course just beyond Anstruther, follow the edge closest to the coast; you are on the public right of way. As you pass the golf course, the trail is obvious and will take you into Pittenweem.

Suggestions for More Walking

The Fife Coast Walk extends 94 miles (151 km) along the North Sea coast from Newburgh through St. Andrews and up to the Forth Road Bridge across from Edinburgh. Although many sections are quite stunning, the trail is not completely developed or waymarked. Sometimes the coastal route can be impassable requiring a long detour on secondary roads. The selection presented above is quite easy to follow and most scenic. If you are looking for a slightly longer variation of this walk, park your car at St. Monance, west of Pittenweem. A shorter option is possible by leaving your car at Anstruther. The same bus passes through all of these towns.

Walk 8: Scotland's Castle Country

Walk: Stonehaven to Dunnotar Castle

50 mins.
2.5 miles (4 km)

General Description

This remote section of Scotland is found on too few tourist lists. Aberdeen, an excellent tourist base, is a gem-like city set along a broad sandy beach extending, north and south, along the usually jagged North Sea coast. Old Aberdeen, a short bus ride from the present city center, preserves its medieval appearance and retains an air of nostalgic tranquility. The walk along historic High Street from fifteenth-century King's College Chapel to fourteenth-century St. Machar's Cathedral will transport you centuries into a stately past. Visit the harbor with its bustling fish market and continue down to Footdee (foot of the River Dee), a tiny fishing community that has yet to be touched by the twentieth century. The business district and the ornate university structures of central Aberdeen also merit a quick ramble.

The surrounding countryside is dotted with dozens of castles and distilleries, and the well-marked, 150-mile Castle Trail (brochure available at the tourist office for this driving tour) will take you through splendid countryside to seven of the most famous of these stone monuments.

The set for Franco Zefferelli's film *Hamlet*, Dunnotar Castle is perched ominously above the crashing waves of the North Sea, surrounded by sheer cliffs on three sides. There is no better walking approach to any castle in Great Britain. The path to the crumbling but still impressive castle affords excellent views of the often angry North Sea and its rugged coast. The air teams with sea gulls and the waters invite neither swimmer nor boater—this is an untamed sea. The castle, standing defiantly against time and a hostile environment, is an eerie sight, particularly on a foggy day. This is definitely an end-of-the-world type of experience as you look out over this vast mistiness into the mysteries of the past.

Optional Maps: Landranger 45/Pathfinder 273

Time/Distance: 50 minutes/2.5 miles (4 km) (including the walk back to the parking lot)

Difficulties: A good climb out of Stonehaven

Toilet Facilities: At Stonehaven and Dunnotar Castle

Refreshments: At Stonehaven and Dunnotar Castle

Getting There: Aberdeen is the usual center for touring the Grampian castles. From Aberdeen, take A92 south to Stonehaven's town center, continuing through to the other side (stop at the tourist office on the main street to pick up a bus schedule or call ahead at Stonehaven 62806) where you can follow the signs to Dunnotar Castle. There is a parking lot at the castle where you can leave your car. Take the bus back to Stonehaven (the stop is just north

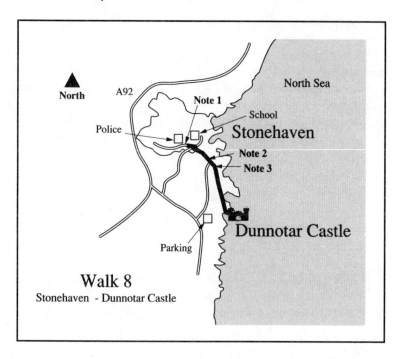

Walk 8
Stonehaven - Dunnotar Castle

of the parking lot) and ask to be let off at the police station. If you are using public transportation, buses run frequently from Aberdeen to Stonehaven; inquire at the bus station. From Stonehaven you may start the walk as described in the trail notes and take the bus back from the castle.

Trail Notes

___ 1. Walk between the police station and the elementary school (ask anyone where the police station is at); continue straight and you will see the path which goes left and up.

___ 2. At the end of the path, go through a fence and turn left onto the road which has a sidewalk.

___ 3. The road will soon turn right, but you will continue straight onto a dirt path. A large war memorial and Dunnotar Castle will be visible

Suggestions for More Walking

There is an abandoned rail line that has been converted to a recreational trail that runs about six miles (9.6 km) from Duthie Park in Aberdeen to the town of Peterculter. The trail parallels a main road where there is frequent bus service back to Aberdeen from almost any point. More adventurous walkers will want to consult the booklet *Hillwalking in the Grampian Highlands*, available at the tourist office in Aberdeen.

Walk 9: Scotland's Whisky Country

Walk: Dufftown (Convalmore Distillery) to Aberlour via the Speyside Way

110 mins. 5.5 miles (8.8 km)

General Description

Dufftown was founded in 1817 by the benevolent James Duff, fourth Earl of Fife, to improve the bleak employment prospects that awaited returning veterans from the Napoleonic wars. The town was well-designed, and remains scarcely changed from its founding decades. This small urban patch centers on the Clock Tower, which harbors "the clock that killed MacPherson." The unfortunate MacPherson, a local version of Robin Hood, was hung when his arch-rival, Lord Braco, who knew there was an impending pardon, set the clock ahead to hasten the execution. The Clock Tower also contains the Dufftown Museum, dedicated primarily to the whisky industry, and the tourist information office. Balvenie Castle, begun in the thirteenth century, can be quickly reached by foot (see the town map available at the tourist office). Just beyond the castle is the Glenfiddich Distillery, which offers tours and samples; but beware: drunken walking is frowned upon in Great Britain.

The path, a short distance from the Glenfiddich distillery, is graced with dense trees, wild flowers, ubiquitous rabbits, and millions of little round rabbit pellets. The land around the trail rolls gracefully, while the trail itself, a former rail bed, is perfectly level—any irregularity, including hills, has been levelled for your convenience. This section of the Speyside Way is just as appropriate for jogging as walking and offers the bonus of being able to view old mile markers and other train signs. First you will follow the narrow but fast moving River Fiddich, which is not always visible, but the tranquilizing sound of water over rocks is always audible. The river has cut a deep valley so that you are often walking along the level of the tree tops, and cows, rendered invisible by the dense forest, communicate in the background. If you wish to relax or have a picnic lunch along the trail, benches are occasionally planted along the route for your convenience at scenic intervals.

Craigellachie, a small town known for its salmon fishing, lies about midway and offers an opportunity for repose and a beverage at the Craigellachie Hotel. Just beyond the town, you will pass through a long, dark, horseshoe-shaped and somewhat ominous looking rail tunnel from the nineteenth century and begin to follow the much wider and faster River Spey, where the deep grass on the river bank, pushed by the wind, appears to be a vast sea of green waves.

Approaching Aberlour, you will note fishermen with boots up to their chests wading in the fast moving waters. Aberlour is a very traditional, attractively organized town with the River Spey on one side and the Conval Hills and Ben Rinnes (a small mountain or tall hill depending on your perspective) on the other side. Virtually all of the structures are gray stone with high pitched roofs, producing a sort of rugged uniformity that fits in well with the frequently somber Scottish skies. A walk along the riverbanks and through the genial town square and a stop in the eccentrically preserved village store will gratify the senses of even the most jaded nostalgia seeker.

Optional Maps: Landranger 28/Pathfinder 180

Time/Distance: 1 hour 50 minutes/5.5 miles (8.8 km)

Difficulties: None

Toilet Facilities: Dufftown, Craigellachie, Aberlour

Refreshments: Dufftown, Craigellachie, Aberlour

Getting There: If you are doing this trail, stay at Aberlour or one of the other small accommodating towns in the area. You can park by the former train station, which is now a tea house and marks the end of today's walk. From Aberlour town center, take the bus (7–8 buses daily with reduced service on Saturday and Sunday: tel. Bluebird Buses, Elgin 544222) to the Convalmore Distillery shortly before it enters Dufftown. (Ask the driver to drop you here, where there are picnic tables and the beginning of the trail is found.) Alternatively, take the bus directly into Dufftown and walk one mile back out to the Convalmore Distillery on A941, where you can to join the trail.

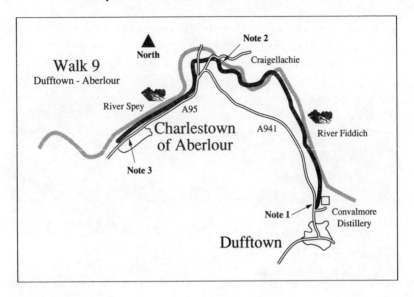

Trail Notes

___ 1. From the bus stop, walk over to the picnic tables and go north along the trail which used to be the path of the train. There is a sign that indicates "Speyside Way."

___ 2. The trail closely bypasses Craigellachie, but you can elect to go up to the village where there are several places to consume beverages and a small store.

___ 3. When you reach the former train station, now tea room, which is clearly marked "Aberlour," you have completed the walk. Stop to have some tea or putt a few holes on the small green before the station for £0.30.

Suggestions for More Walking

The Speyside Way follows the River Spey for thirty miles from Tugnet on the Spey Bay to Ballindalloch and then proceeds another fifteen miles through forested hills to Tomintoul. (An informative map/brochure can be ordered for £0.50 from the following address: The Ranger, Boat O'Fiddich, Graigellachie, Banffshire,

Scotland. Telephone (01343-543451). The entire trail is both scenic and accessible via the Speyside Rambler, a bus that traverses
the trail route on Sundays, Wednesdays, and Fridays from early
June through late September (schedule also available from The
Ranger, or contact G.B. Gray, Castle Street, Fochabers, Scotland;
telephone (01343-820518). This pristine, lightly touristed area is
worth a three-day visit, and you could easily do a different walk
each day.

Walk 10: Scottish Highlands

Walk: Altnafeadh to Kinlochleven via the West Highland Way

General Description

140 mins. 6.5 miles (10.5 km)

The Scottish Highlands embody the
ideal of rugged beauty. Characterized by serrated peaks, tempestuous coastal terrain, and often ethereal loneliness, the Highlands
are best explored on foot. The Glencoe Valley between Oban and
Fort William is a microcosm of the general area, with sinister
summits concealing pacific mountain lakes and offering million-
dollar views for the the price of a few buckets of perspiration.
Enjoy the rugged, healthy atmosphere. This is one of the few trails
in Great Britain where you will see backpackers, and the Scottish
Highlands have the sort of athletic ambiance encountered in the
Rocky Mountain states or the European Alps.

Today's walk begins at Altnafeadh, a wide spot in the road
catering mainly to mountaineers and others who wish to attain
the "look" of a mountaineer. Not much to delay you here except
the views in all directions.

As you ascend from Altnafeadh, you will be accompanied by
the pleasant sound of fresh mountain water over rocks—or is that
the sound of perspiration pouring out of your overworked body?
The almost directly vertical climb upward is probably the most

difficult in this book, and when you reach the top of what is aptly called the "Devil's Staircase" (dubbed so by soldiers forced to traverse this eighteenth-century military road), you will have had a thirty-minute aerobic workout. When no other walkers are visible, it is a lonely mountainous place. Dark, forboding peaks are visible in the distance. Atmospheric conditions change quickly, revealing a variety of panoramic views with the sun occasionally piercing the mist. Waterproof boots are a good idea; shallow streams must be forded. This is the area described by Robert Louis Stevenson in *Kidnapped*, and there is no finer walk through the Scottish Highlands. However, civilization is gradually encroaching even into remote mountain fastnesses. Not far from Kinlochleven, still high in the mountains, a sign has been erected that bears this message: "Kenstock Cottage: Proposed tea room—If there was a tea room at the cottage behind this notice would you stop for refreshments?" You are offered a Yes or No button and your vote is electronically tallied while a colored light blinks. I have mixed emotions concerning the above-mentioned enterprise but I did vote yes, since I would have stopped for a beverage at such a magnificent location. Kinlochleven is a center for the processing of aluminum and has a small display and audio-visual program about aluminum at the visitors' center. The Alcan plant itself appears to be the sort of Industrial Revolution sweatshop a Dickens character would somberly emerge from after an eighteen-hour day. The town, however, is pleasantly situated in a valley at the western end of Loch Leven and offers the possibility of dining and overnight accommodations.

Optional Maps: Landranger 41/Outdoor Leisure 8

Time/Distance: 2 hours 20 minutes/6.5 miles (10.5 km)

Difficulties: Initial thirty minutes uphill followed by other less difficult ascents; long descent into Kinlochleven

Toilet Facilities: Only at Kinlochleven, some privacy on the trail

Refreshments: At Kinlochleven

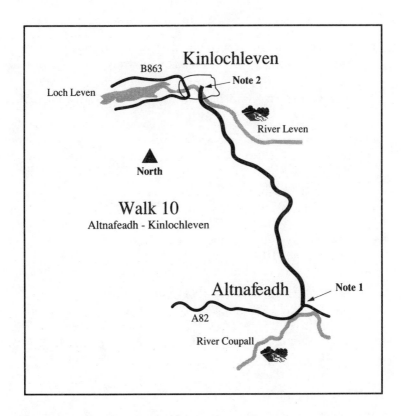

Getting There: From Fort William, drive south to North Ballachulish on A82 where you will turn left onto B863 and continue to Kinlochleven; alternatively, there are frequent buses from Fort William to Kinlochleven. From Kinlochleven, take the bus (several per day, none Sunday: telephone Highland Bus and Coach in Fort William (01397-702373) to Glencoe Crossroads (back to A82). From Glencoe Crossroads, you will take another bus to Altnafeadh. If you are in a hurry, call Mr. Cameron, proprietor of Kinlochleven Taxis (who also runs a B&B) at Kinlochleven 656, who will take you from Kinlochleven to Altnafeadh and tell you about the trail, which he has walked (£12).

Trail Notes

___ 1. When you emerge from the bus or taxi, you will observe a public footpath sign which leads you straight up. From this point, the trail is obvious until you reach Kinlochleven.

___ 2. When you reach Kinlochleven, walk on the road behind the plant which takes you into town.

Suggestions for More Walking

The West Highland Way traverses 95 miles (153 km) of Scotland's finest scenery from the outskirts of Glasgow to Fort William. The trail alternates between tranquil facility and terrifying difficulty but there is no moment of longing to be elsewhere. The official guide is *The West Highland Way* by Robert Aitken. The final stage of the south-to-north trek along the West Highland Way begins at Kinlochleven and terminates at Fort William. This is a beautiful but often difficult fourteen-mile trek that cannot be broken into more manageable segments. Start early, take the bus from Fort William to Kinlochleven, bring a lunch, and do not be in a hurry. There are numerous circular walks in the area, particularly around Scotland's tallest peak, Ben Nevis. Information is available at the Fort William tourist office.

Walk 11: Glasgow/Loch Lomond

Walk: **Ardlui to the Drover's Inn at Inverarnan via the West Highland Way**

75 mins.
3.2 miles (5.1 km)

General Description

If you are sojourning in Glasgow or merely passing through on the way north, you must spend a day around Loch Lomond, one of Britain's largest (23 miles/37 km long) and most beautiful lakes. There are numerous sites, including Balloch Castle with its beautiful grounds and the cave of Rob Roy (rogue/hero immortalized by Sir Walter Scott in his novel *Rob Roy*) which can be reached by foot about one mile north of Inversnaid.

The lake region also serves as a mini-paradise for the athletically inclined, offering cycling, fishing, golf, sailing, water skiing, swimming, and, of course, hiking. Tourist offices at Dumbarton, Balloch, Tarbet, and Drymen are capable of delivering pounds of information on this region. The attractive towns in this area also offer comfortable lodging and fine regional dining, which may entice you to linger for a while.

Today's adventure begins at Ardlui on the quieter, often more scenic, and less touristed northern shores of the lake. Small and unpretentious, Ardlui has a hotel and several restaurants. Nothing seems to happen here, but you will appreciate the change in atmosphere if you have passed the day(s) around the more popular southern lake shores. From the harbor, a short ferry ride (actually a launch that caters to walkers) takes you directly across the lake to a world without vehicular traffic—there are no roads on this side of the lake, and the tranquility found here could not be had in several bottles of Valium. As the ferry recedes into the background, you will begin to climb above the lake into a timbered, green world where only the walker can go. Views of the lake are outstanding but soon disappear as you begin to trace the course of the swift-running River Falloch. As you descend from the hills and cross the river you will soon be at Inverarnan, a delightful extension of nowhere that harbors one of the finest trail ends in Britain, the Drover's Inn. This proud pub, established in 1701, has welcomed wayfarers for almost three centuries and makes no attempt to conceal its age—you will expect horse-drawn carriages to halt noisily at its entrance hastily discharging parched characters from a Sir Walter Scott novel. After the Scott characters are herded back into their carriages, slip out of the pub through a rear door and inspect the small menagerie of animals protected by the owner, including a free-roving peacock with expansive plumage.

Optional Maps: Landranger 56/Pathfinder 357

Time/Distance: 1 hour 15 minutes/3.2 miles (5.1 km)

Difficulties: Some climbing

Toilet Facilities: At Ardlui and the Drover's Inn

Refreshments: At Ardlui and the Drover's Inn

Getting There: From Glasgow, take A82 north along the west coast of Loch Lomond to the Drover's Inn at Inverarnan. From Inverarnan, take the bus back to Ardlui; ask the driver to drop you at the Marina. Skye-Ways operates three per day (tel. 0141-33242100) and Citylinking operates four per day (tel. 0141-3329191). Schedules will also be available at most tourist offices in the area. At Ardlui, take the ferry (7 per day, May through August) across Loch Lomond where you will begin the walk. By public transportation from Glasgow, take the bus to Ardlui. The buses mentioned above both originate in Glasgow.

Trail Notes

___ 1. From the ferry, walk to the left. You will see a gate that will take you to the trail where you continue north. From this point, the trail is obvious.

___ 2. To return to Inverarnan, you will turn left and follow the course of a stream back to the road. The left turn to Inverarnan is clearly marked. You will cross a wooden bridge over the the river. When you reach the road (A82) turn left and you will be back at the Drover's Inn in a few minutes.

Suggestions for More Walking

The West Highland Way is described above in Walk 10. For walkers looking to enjoy a longer walk, it is easy to continue beyond Inverarnan and up to Crianlarich (6 miles/9.6 km). If you opt for

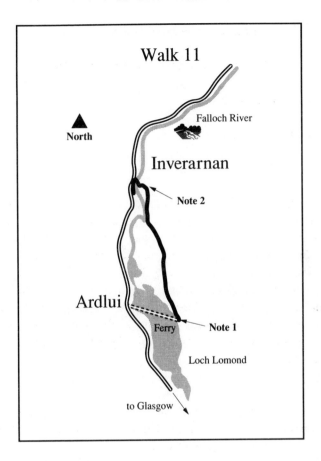

Walk 11

North

Falloch River

Inverarnan

Note 2

Ardlui

Ferry — Note 1

Loch Lomond

to Glasgow

this longer version, leave your car at Crianlarich and take the Scotrail steam train called the West Highland Line (and billed as "one of the great railway journeys of the world") to Ardlui for the ferry. The official Scotrail guide to the line is available at all local tourist offices and train stations. This guide also makes a number of suggestions for walks that can be done in conjunction with the train. Also useful, if you will be in the region for a while, is the Bartholomew guide *Walk Loch Lomond and the Trossachs*, which is a compendium of 35 circular walks in the area.

Walk 12: South Scotland's Atlantic Coast

Walk: **Portpatrick to Stranraer via the Southern Upland Way**

200 mins.
9 miles (14.5 km)

General Description

This southernmost area of Scotland managed to win freedom from England in the early fourteenth century under the leadership of the region's most favorite son, Robert the Bruce. Although not very touristed, this region is a visual delight, combining miles of rugged coastline with rolling green hills and desolate expanses of moorland to quickly captivate the observant wayfarer.

Today's trek introduces you to the Galloway area in all of its diversity. Beginning at a traditional Scottish fishing village, the trail takes in a couple of miles of rugged coastline, a working lighthouse, variegated farmland, and an extensive heather moor, until finally terminating at a bustling seaport.

Tiny Portpatrick belies its size by climbing high on the slopes overlooking the bay. This verticality gives the town an appearance of being a much greater metropolis. Tourists will find every sort of amenity from good lodging to fine dining, but the town life is still dominated by the fishermen who, daily in small boats, challenge the immense ocean. The walk begins on the high cliffs overlooking the raging Atlantic Ocean. The screams of high-flying sea gulls are barely heard over the fierce crashing of waters onto the cliffs. After about two miles of such pulse-quickening trekking you will arrive at the still functioning Black Head lighthouse, which continues to guide fishermen home through threatening mists and choppy waters. Leaving the coast, you will set off on a remote inland route to Stranraer. Here, on the narrow asphalt road that takes you from the lighthouse, cows graze with impunity. You will pass through numerous fields, skirt a small lake, and traverse an extensive moor region that seems to have been painted in fall colors. The lonely moors are both bleak and spectacular, offering some of the finest walking in Great Britain. The first views of Stranraer are impressive; from a lofty promontory the entire expanse of this industrious port is spread before your eyes. You will now descend into a major port, home of the ferry to Northern Ireland. Actually, Stranraer is rather sedate and gracious in its welcome. There is not much here to hold you for more than a day. However, there are abundant accommodations and the walk combined with the general ambience of an ocean seaport make this worth an overnight stay. Take the time to visit the 75-acre Castle Kennedy Gardens, which are located close enough to reach on foot (see Suggestions for More Walking). The castle itself, destroyed by fire in the early eighteenth century, stands romantically enveloped by the magnificent foliage and flowers that bloom everywhere throughout the gardens.

Optional Maps: Landranger 82/Pathfinder 537, 538, 551

Time/Distance: 3 hours 20 minutes/9 miles (14.5 km)

Difficulties: Some difficult coastal walking and climbing

Toilet Facilities: At Portpatrick and Stranraer, but much privacy on the trail beyond the coastal portion

Refreshments: Portpatrick and Stranraer

Getting There: Completion of this walk will probably involve a night in Stranraer or Portpatrick. If you stay at Stranraer, take the bus (#67, 4–7 per day) to Portpatrick's harbor. If you stay at Portpatrick, follow the trail notes and return via bus.

Trail Notes

___ 1. As you stand in Portpatrick's harbor facing the ocean, look to the right; at the end of the harbor you will see an information kiosk for the Southern Upland Way. Behind the kiosk there is a staircase that marks the beginning of the trail.

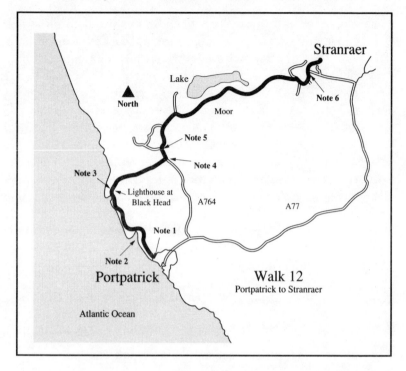

Walk 12
Portpatrick to Stranraer

___ 2. After about 20 minutes, you will cross a small sandy beach. At the other end, you will go left almost immediately.

___ 3. When you reach the lighthouse's small parking lot, turn right on the narrow asphalt road that leads away from it.

___ 4. When you come to an intersecting asphalt road, turn left (after about one hour twenty minutes).

___ 5. About four or five minutes later, you will see a signpost directing you down another narrow asphalt road to your right.

___ 6. When you reach the outskirts of Stranraer (2 hours 50 minutes), you will see a signpost that directs you to the right. However, at this point, you can look down into the valley and see Stranraer. Ignore the signpost and walk straight ahead and downhill. When you see the church, continue in that direction towards the harbor.

Suggestions for More Walking

The Southern Upland Way begins at Portpatrick in the west and proceeds to cross Scotland in a easterly direction until, 212 miles (341 km) later, it terminates at Cockburnspath east of Edinburgh. The official guides, *The Southern Upland Way*, 2 vols., HMSO, 1984, have been written by Ken Andrew. The Southern Upland Way continues out of Stranraer and over to beautiful Castle Kennedy about four miles (6.5 km) to the east. This is an attractive walk that has an excellent destination. Buses run frequently between these two points and the walk can be done in either direction. From Portpatrick a two-mile (3.2 km) coastal round trip to Dunskey Castle is well worth the time invested. The castle is in spectacular ruins and the walk will take you along the wonderfully untamed coastal scenery to the south of Portpatrick.

Walk 13: Northern Lake District

Walk: **Grange to Keswick via the Cumbria Way**

120 mins.
5.2 miles (8.4 km)

General Description

The Lake District, largest and most visited of Britain's national parks, is an aggregation of sharp peaks, rounded hills, woodland, farmland, and enchantingly beautiful valley lakes. This is one of Britain's finest walking regions, with excellent accommodations throughout. This walk finds its terminus in Keswick on the banks of lovely Derwent Water, an excellent choice for a base of operations. However, Windermere, Ambleside, Grasmere, and numerous smaller towns in between are all equally attractive and convenient.

The trail begins at Grange, a pretty village with several B&Bs, a store, and two small churches. You could decode the key to total tranquility by establishing a base here. The trail through Grange begins on a charming asphalt road lined with stone fences. Grazing sheep, goats, and cattle are ubiquitous and cacaphonous. Mistenshrouded hills rise to your left, and as you ascend from Grange, sterling views of Derwent Water and Keswick are beheld in the distance. After a long trek through the high country, you will descend and enter a shimmering, emerald-green forest. Secluded woodland paths, skirting the lake, will guide you into Keswick, where all of the advantages and few of the negatives associated with civilization await.

Optional Maps: Landranger 89/Outdoor Leisure 4

Time/Distance: 2 hours/5.2 miles (8.4 km)

Difficulties: Several climbs

Toilet Facilities: Grange, Keswick; some privacy

Refreshments: Grange, Keswick

Getting There: From the Keswick bus station, take bus #79 to the Grange Bridge (7 per day).

Trail Notes

___ 1. From the bus stop, walk over the bridge and into the village of Grange.

___ 2. Continue along the asphalt road as it winds through the town.

___ 3a. After about 17 minutes, you will see a public footpath signpost that directs you to the left and up.

___ 3b. A couple of minutes later, you will come to a point where it appears that you can go in several different directions. Climb over the fence where steps are provided.

___ 4. You come to a fork where you have the option of rising steeply or rising, but not so steeply. Unless you feel like a good climb, take the lower path. However, both meet at approximately the same place, and both offer excellent views.

___ 5. When you arrive at an asphalt road (about 35 minutes),

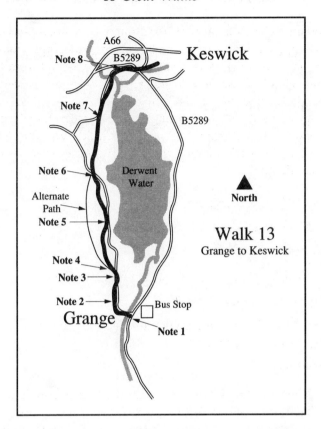

Note 8
A66
B5289
Keswick

Note 7

B5289

Note 6
Derwent
Water

▲
North

Alternate
Path
Note 5

Walk 13
Grange to Keswick

Note 4
Note 3

Note 2
Bus Stop
Grange
Note 1

climb to your left in a couple of minutes (or, if you prefer, continue along the asphalt road which the trail eventually joins again).

___ 6a. When you reach the asphalt road, follow it briefly. You will see a signpost directing you into the forest.

___ 6b. When you reach a fork a couple of minutes later, go left.

___ 7. When you reach the next asphalt road follow it to your right into Keswick.

___ 8. When you cross the bridge, look to the right for the well-marked footpath that will lead you into Keswick.

Suggestions for More Walking

The Cumbria Way is a 76-mile (122 km), north-to-south trail that makes its way through some of the most attractive terrain of the Lake District. The most recent guide is John Trevelyan's *The Cumbria Way*, third edition, Dalesman, 1987. You can join this portion of the Cumbria Way at several points along Derwent Water by taking the Keswick-on-Derwent-Water Launch, which runs on a regular schedule to a variety of points on the lakeshore (schedules available at the tourist office). For a longer, more difficult walk, try the Allerdale Ramble, which is an approximately eight-mile (13 km), circular hike through the hills from Keswick (information available at the tourist office).

Walk 14: Southern Lake District

Walk: Ravenglass to Muncaster Mill

90 mins.
4 miles (6.4 km)

General Description

An excellent two-day sojourn in the Lake District could involve a stay at Keswick and Walk 13 above on the first day with the next day dedicated to this beautiful walk.

Today's adventure begins with a ride on a miniature steam train. The Ravenglass and Eskdale Railway, "one of the greatest little trains of the world," has been serving as transportation in this remote section of the Lake District since 1876. It began as a mining train to bring ore from Eskdale to the main line at Ravenglass and quickly added passenger cars. Several times service was suspended only to be revived by railway enthusiasts; currently, revenues have been sufficient for substantial restoration, and if you have the time, take in the entire seven-mile (11.2 km) ride.

You will board the train at the Muncaster Mill where flour was first ground in 1455. The water-powered mill is still functioning, and it is possible to purchase traditional stone-ground flour and oatmeal. After a short, lively jaunt you will arrive at Ravenglass, which was a Roman port called Clanoventa. Currently, this most attractive small town is the home of the Ravenglass and Eskdale Railway with its station, workshops, pub, and museum. A stroll through the railway area and town is well worth a few minutes pause before embarking along the trail.

Along the woodland trail, you will quickly arrive at Walls Castle, the tallest Roman ruin in Great Britain, which can be reached only on foot. Actually, what remains is the bath house from the fort, which scholars believe the Romans constructed in anticipation of the never fulfilled conquest of Ireland. From Walls Castle, a short, pleasant walk will take you to Muncaster Castle, home of the Pennington family since the thirteenth century. The castle is open to the public and a short tour will take you through a variety of medieval rooms, including a reputedly haunted bedroom. Watch for the portrait of Thomas Skelton, the last Fool of Muncaster, who gave the English language the word "tomfoolery." The gardens, a combination of wild and groomed beauty, are extensive; a complete visit will add about two miles to your walk. Also on the grounds is the Muncaster Owl Center, which boasts one of the finest collections of owls in the world. The owls are well cared for, and visitors will be astonished at the diversity of this species. If you are lucky, they will hiss at you. There is a daily "Meet the Birds" show at 2:30 p.m., and video cameras are installed in some nests to allow visitors the luxury of observing the private lives of these unusual creatures. From the grounds of Muncaster Castle, it is a short forested walk back to Muncaster Mill and refreshments.

Optional Maps: Landranger 96/Outdoor Leisure 6

Time/Distance: 1 hour 30 minutes/4 miles (6.4 km)

Difficulties: None

Toilet Facilities: Ravenglass, Muncaster Castle, Muncaster Mill

Refreshments: Ravenglass, Muncaster Castle, Muncaster Mill

Getting There: Ravenglass is in the southwestern section of the Lake District on A595. By car from Keswick, drive east on A66 and then south on A595 just before Workington. If you arrive from the north on A595, look for the signs just before arrival in Ravenglass that indicate the turn for the Muncaster Mill, which is just off A595. Arriving from the south, bypass Ravenglass and look for the Muncaster Mill signs. Buses and trains run to Ravenglass from a variety of locations in the Lake District. From Muncaster Mill, take the steam train to Ravenglass. Trains run hourly during June and early July and every twenty to 40 minutes during late July and August. The train runs throughout the rest of the year, but less frequently (tel. (01229-717171).

Trail Notes

___ 1a. At the end of Ravenglass' train platform where the device that turns the trains is located, you will see a bridge spanning the tracks.

___ 1b. Walk up the path that leads to the bridge and turn left. You do not cross the bridge.

___ 1c. Minutes later you will come to a gate where you will turn right. There is a public footpath signpost indicating "Newton Knott and Muncaster."

___ 2. Just beyond the Roman bath house, the trail bifurcates. Go left down the dirt path. Do not continue to your right on the asphalt road.

___ 3. Turn left when you see the first public footpath sign.

___ 4. Follow the trail to the road (A595), and turn right. You will soon be at the main gate of Muncaster Castle.

___ 5. After visiting Muncaster Castle, turn right as you emerge from the gate, and continue along the road (A595) until it turns sharply right. At this point you will turn left where you see a trail and public footpath sign. This will take you to Muncaster Mill.

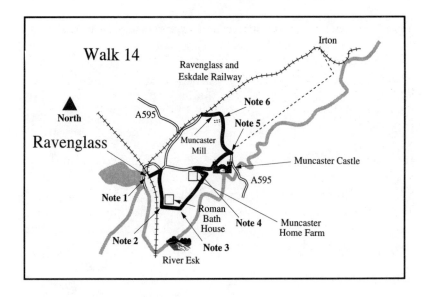

___ 6. Just before Muncaster Mill, the trail bifurcates. You will continue straight, avoiding the sharp left.

Suggestions for More Walking

For a longer walk (add about three difficult miles), leave your car at either the Irton Station or Eskdale Green and walk back along the Muncaster Fell (fell=high, rocky wasteland). This lonely trek adds new meaning to the phrase "lonely at the top." If you select this option, just continue straight ahead where A595 turns right and the trail to Muncaster Mill goes left. There is a public bridleway sign. This trail can be very muddy; wear sturdy boots. Although there are few markers, it is difficult to become seriously lost since the trail stays to the right of the peaks on this narrow promontory (although I did have visions of some archaeologist finding my body in a bog 2000 years from now and wondering what the hell I was doing up here). Bring a good map. When you dead end at a stone wall that you cannot miss, turn left and the path will lead you to the Irton Station. Alternatively, you could take the train from the main station at Ravenglass south to the Bootle station and walk back along the Cumbria Cycle Way. This circa six-mile walk will take you along the coast overlooking the ocean and extensive dunes (you are warned to stay off the dunes and on the trail). The trail is easy to follow and clearly marked on the O.S. Outdoor Leisure map #6, but Bootle station does not appear since it is just south of the map's edge. However it does appear on Landranger map #96.

Walk 15: Ribble Valley/Blackpool

Walk: **Sawley Abbey to Clitheroe via the Ribble Way**

General Description

135 mins.
6 miles (9.6 km)

Blackpool is Britain's version of Co-ney Island, a working-class resort with a seven-mile (11 km) promenade along the ocean and enough junk-food indigestion to make you wish you had remembered your Alka-Seltzer. Actually, Blackpool, with its infinite beaches, gaudy lighting, and low-brow entertainment is worth a short excursion and can be justified as a low-culture experience. However, unless you are a professional video game player, 2–3 hours in Blackpool will be sufficient. The Ribble River Valley is an hour away from Blackpool (via M55, M6, and A59) by car but light years away in ambience. Here is a truly tranquil and untouristed part of Great Britain, and Clitheroe, with its retinue of diminutive satellite towns, offers a pacific alternative to a sojourn in frenetic Blackpool.

Today's walk begins at Sawley, a charming riverside town composed of ivy-covered cottages surrounded by proper and plush English gardens. There is not much traffic here, and geese amble contentedly down the main street unmolested by vehicular traffic. They do not deign to move for the occasional automobile; drivers must negotiate curbs in order to give the geese due respect and a right of way. The medieval abbey is Sawley's main attraction, and a stop at this elegant ruin will transport you quickly into England's medieval past.

Ascending from town, you will join the River Ribble as it moves swiftly along its rocky bed surrounded by an intensely green and undulating valley. Distant views of the river and its valley are spectacular. The trail hugs the riverbank throughout much of the walk, and as you approach Clitheroe, the atmosphere becomes park-like with benches placed at scenic and convenient intervals. Bring a picnic lunch or simply graze with the sheep for a while on the fine green grass that lines the river banks.

Clitheroe is a gem-like town tucked away in this green valley along the banks of the river, and a visit to the well-preserved castle in the town center makes a fine conclusion to a superb walk.

Optional Maps: Landranger 103/Pathfinder 669

Time/Distance: 2 hours 15 minutes/6 miles (9.6 km)

Difficulties: Some minor climbs

Toilet Facilities: Sawley, Clitheroe; much privacy

Refreshments: Restaurants and stores at Sawley and Clitheroe

Getting There: If you are staying in Blackpool, take M55 to M6 south. You will then take the first exit at Blackburn and proceed east on A677. When the road forks, take A59 to the left (northeast) to Clitheroe. At Clitheroe, take the 280 bus in the direction of Skipton from the Wells Terrace Station to Sawley, which runs every 1–2 hours. The bus does not enter Sawley; ask the driver to drop you at the road leading to the abbey. By public transportation, take the bus from Blackpool to Preston, where you switch for the 280 bus to Sawley.

Trail Notes

___ 1. From the bus stop walk north to the river along the road about $\frac{1}{4}$ mile to the abbey.

___ 2. Visit the abbey and continue along the road. When you come to the end of the abbey road, turn left by the Spread Eagle Hotel along the asphalt road which crosses the river.

___ 3. As you cross the bridge, look to your left; you will see a stile that takes you along the river. If you prefer, you may simply continue down the road since the trail joins it again in a few minutes. When you rejoin the road, turn left.

___ 4a. After about 25 minutes you will have almost completed your ascent out of Sawley. You will see a school to your right and a couple of other buildings. After you pass these buildings, begin to look left. When the road curves right, you will see a public footpath sign that leads you left and down to the river.

___ 4b. As you descend, look for a stile at the far end of the field where the wire fence meets the stone wall. After crossing the stile, walk to the riverbank and turn right.

___ 5a. Walk along the river path until you come to a bridge which you will cross over the river.

___ 5b. Continue south along the road. Ignore the public footpath sign to your left; just beyond it you will see a public foot-
___ path sign and Ribble Way sign indicating "West Bradford $1\frac{1}{4}$ miles"

___ 6. Once in the park, having reached a vehicular road, turn left and into Clitheroe.

Suggestions for More Walking

The Ribble Way extends 72 miles (116 km) from its source near Horton-in-Ribblesdale to its estuary near Preston. The entire walk is described in Gladys Sellers' *The Ribble Way*, Cicerone Press, 1992. Another shorter (about four miles), but equally attractive, walk along the Ribble River is between Gisburne with its attractive park and Sawley Abbey. For an extended walk, begin at Gisburne and continue on to Clitheroe. The bus service mentioned above continues along to Gisburne. A bonus for the walker who visits Blackpool is the inexpensive tramway that follows the beach promenade

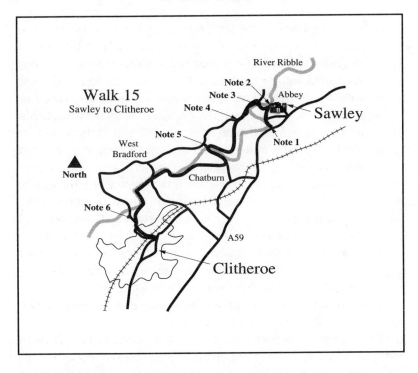

for seven miles, making it possible to walk as far as endurance allows and return to any point in town by the tram.

Walk 16: Peak District

Walk: **Miller's Dale to Castleton via the Limestone Way** (Note: Public Transportation for this walk is available only on Sundays; however, this is an excellent area for hiking, and several guides detail circular walks from this area)

170 mins.
7.5 miles (12 km)

General Description

The Peak District National Park, one of the largest parks in Britain, covers almost 550 square miles. Circumscribed within this immensity is an undulating terrain consisting of incisor-like gray hills, barren pasture lands, paths lined with tall, stone-constructed walls, and intermittent woodlands with the occasional isolated village thrown in. Sweeping views of broad expanses and low-lying peaks will enhance your walk throughout.

Miller's Dale, liliputian in scale but picturesquely situated, radiates Peak District quaintness. Take some time to linger along the banks of the River Wye as it cuts a swift path through the town—bring a picnic lunch or relax at the riverside tavern. As you depart Miller's Dale, enjoy the peerless views of the River Wye and its valley. Having climbed out of the valley, you will enter a narrow path encompassed by stone walls dividing lengthy fields of brilliant wild flowers. The diminutive, enclosed fields encountered along the trail are remnants of the Middle Ages, a time when land was continually divided among heirs resulting in today's patchwork of narrow fields.

Soon into the walk, you will come upon the beautifully maintained turn-of-the-century Monksdale House, a sign of the prosperity that still lingers in some rural areas of England. Beyond the Monksdale House, you will traverse a long, narrow valley called Peter's Dale. Here, limestone cliffs tower over the dense foliage of the fertile valley forming a quiet, shady respite from the sun. Rabbits, ears down, flatten themselves along the valley floor trying to appear as brown rocks. When you have ascended from the valley you will enjoy magnificent views of this enchanted dale.

The approach to Castleton is graced by the formidable Peveril Castle. Built by William Peveril, bastard son of William the Conqueror, the fortress still stands mightily on its lofty crag and merits a visit. The descent in this area is steep and rocky; caution is advised.

Castleton, one of the most popular and attractive towns in the Peak District, welcomes numerous visitors with its stores, B&Bs, restaurants, and scenic beauty. Castleton's main attractions, beyond its ambience, are a group of encircling caverns. Trails link these subterranean treasures, and Blue John Cavern is renowned for its eponymous feldspar. This purplish-blue stone is unique in the world and also sold in many local emporiums.

Optional Maps: Landranger 110, 116/Outdoor Leisure 1, 24

Time/Distance: 2 hours 50 minutes/7.5 miles (12km)

Difficulties: Frequent climbs

Toilet Facilities: Miller's Dale, Castleton; frequent privacy

Refreshments: Miller's Dale (pub), Castleton (pubs, stores, restaurants)

Getting There: By car: Castleton lies about midway between Manchester and Sheffield along A625. However, traffic is slow in this area and spending the night in Castleton is not a bad idea. From Castleton, Mainline bus 181 departs only on summer Sundays and bank holiday Mondays at 11:20 a.m. (tel. Sheffield (01742-561144). Ask the driver to drop you at Miller's Dale. Wealthy travellers can call a taxi from Hope about $1\frac{1}{2}$ miles from Castleton (tel. (01433-620221 or 620732). *By Public Transportation*: Several Mainline daily buses (#272) from Sheffield Interchange will deliver you to Castleton if you wish to spend the night. If you are in Sheffield on a Sunday and have been lusting for a day in the Peaks, take Mainline bus #181 to Miller's Dale in the morning, walk to Castleton, have lunch, and take the late afternoon bus back to Sheffield.

Trail Notes

__ 1a. At Miller's Dale the bus drops you off at the church. You will see a public footpath sign next to the church: do not follow this path.

__ 1b. Walk back on the road that the bus took until you see a narrow road going up a hill. You will see an arrow and a

ram's head, which is the symbol for the Limestone Way.
Walk up this road.

__ 2. After about 18 minutes (you will be still walking down a
trail surrounded by stone walls on both sides), you will
come to a junction; turn left at this point.

__ 3. About 25 minutes into the walk, you will reach a junction
and see the Monksdale House. Turn left here onto an asphalt road; there is a Limestone Way sign to guide you.

__ 4. Continue along the asphalt road for about ten minutes, looking to your right. You will see a Limestone Way sign directing you onto a path.

__ 5. Continuing along the valley, turn right when you cross over
a stile and reach the second road that intersects with the
trail (actually a broad trail between two stone fences).

__ 6. When you reach an asphalt road, turn left onto the road.
Ignore the public footpath sign that takes you into the field.

__ 7a. When you reach the next road (A623, a rather busy thoroughfare), cross to the other side and turn left. Begin to
look right; a couple of minutes later, you will turn right
down a path which is not marked (it is a gated, two-track
path with stone fences on both sides).

__ 7b. Continue straight along this former railway track, ignoring a public footpath sign to your left. (Also ignore the
sign indicating Tideswell/Bradwell.) You will eventually
see a sign indicating Castleton.

__ 8a. After about 2 hours 20 minutes, you will pass through a
gate where you sill see an interesting broad trail. Then you
will pass through another gate where you will see an arrow directing you to your right.

__ 8b. A few minutes beyond the gate, the trail divides. Do not
go straight ahead and over the hill (although this route
also goes to Castleton); go right and downhill along a broad
but faint path that goes through an old metal gate. You
will soon pass Peveril Castle. The descent around the castle
is quite steep and rocky so pay attention to your footing.

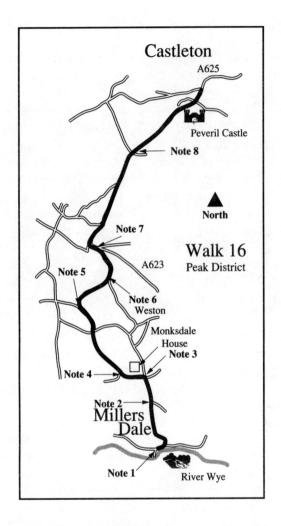

Suggestions for More Walking

The Limestone Way extends 26 miles through the Peak District National Park from Matlock to Castleton. A brochure describing this walk is available from the West Derbyshire District Council, Town Hall, Bank Road, Matlock, Derbyshire DE4 3NN. Given the

paucity of public transportation in this area, it is not possible to recommend variations of this particular walk; however, there are many circular walks in this area. In particular, the walks to the caverns around Castleton are worthwhile and not very lengthy. The National Park Information Center in Castleton has a variety of useful publications.

Walk 17: Northern Wales/ Snowdonia

Walk: **Groeslon to Caernarfon Castle via the Lon Eifion**

90 mins.
4.5 miles (7.2 km)

General Description

Indomitable in their intent to main-
tain cultural differentiation from England, the Welsh resist assimi-

lation and cling tenaciously to their Celtic language and traditional culture. If this is your first stop in Wales, you will be surprised to note that the Welsh language is spoken far more frequently than English, although most Welsh are also conversant in the Queen's language. Wales does not disappoint. The rugged coastline, often sublime terrain, and multitudinous remnants of the distant past combine with the Welsh tradition of solicitous care for the tourist to ensure a genial and riveting sojourn.

Caernarfon, where today's enterprise commences, must be the bus capital of Wales or perhaps the universe. Buses of all sizes, shapes, and colors sputter in and out in endless procession producing an almost toxic atmosphere. However, once seated you will soon be transported out of the internal-combustion-engine-induced haze into a tableau of quiet verdancy.

Soon you will arrive at Groeslon, nowhere in particular, but pleasant enought to stop for a drink before zipping back to Caernarfon. The trail, an abandoned railway line, is level and partially paved. In the world of trails, this is a superhighway. The path is sheltered by dense stands of deciduous trees and graced with an effusion of wild flowers throughout its length. Along some portions of the trail the great tides of the Atlantic Ocean are revealed while along other sections the nobility of the ocean stands in contrast to the rusting, uninhabitable but still inhabited trailer homes that attest to the lingering poverty of this region.

The views of the enormous and well-preserved castle as you enter Caernarfon are astonishing and these particular views are only available to walkers. A cavernous, gray hulk, Caernarfon Castle has stood impregnable since the thirteenth century. Constructed by Edward I as a stronghold against Welsh liberation, this multi-turreted redoubt has stood tall against redoubtable opponents throughout the centuries and continues its life as one of the finest souvenirs of the European Middle Ages. Wander and climb about the fortress or take one of the hourly tours. Your time will be well spent.

The city surrounding the castle is also worth a brief sojourn.

Inspect the substantial remnants of the walls that encircled the city in more turbulent times, and procure Welsh artifacts along attractive pedestrian thoroughfares. Accommodations are abundant and economical. Finally, on the southeastern outskirts of the city along route A4085 is the Roman fort Segontium, one of the most famous Roman ruins in Britain. Overlooking Caernarfon, this monument to Roman tenacity, with its modern museum, serves as a time warp into the distant past.

Optional Maps: Landranger 115/Outdoor Leisure 17

Time/Distance: 90 minutes/4.5 miles (7.2 km)

Difficulties: None

Toilet Facilities: Groeslon, Caernarfon; some privacy

Refreshments: Groeslon, Caernarfon, Goat Hotel at the junction with A499

Getting There: Buses (#1 or #80) run hourly from Caernarfon's Castle Square to Groeslon. Schedules, which change often and seem to bear little relation to reality, are available at the tourist office. Ask the driver to drop you at Groeslon and be vigilant in watching for the town yourself; the driver may forget.

Trail Notes

___ 1a. From the bus stop walk to the post office, which is at the town's only crossroads.

___ 1b. From the post office, walk across the street. You will turn right almost immediately where you see the trail, which is an abandoned railway line running parallel with the A487.

___ 2. When come to the first road (A499), cross, go to your right, and in about 100 yards you will see the path where you turn left. From this point, there is no difficulty in following the trail to Caernarfon.

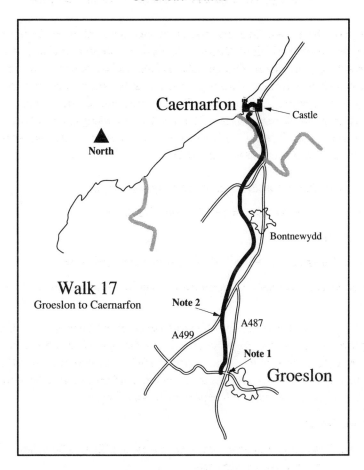

Walk 17
Groeslon to Caernarfon

Suggestions for More Walking

Lon Eifion (Eifion's Way) follows a south/north 21-mile (34 km) route from Cricieth on the Tremadog Bay to Caernarfon on the Caernarfon Bay. A bilingual (Welsh/English) brochure is available from the Planning Department, Gwynedd County Council, Caernarfon, Gwynedd LL55 1SH. The trail parallels a major road (A487/B4411) throughout its length, and transportation to and from all points is frequent. Overnight accommodations and dining opportunities are also available at convenient intervals. This walk can be shortened to two miles by taking the bus to Bontnewydd, where you can also join the trail, or conveniently lengthened to seven miles by taking the bus to Penygroes. Or you may start from any other point along the bus route to Cricieth. Another popular excursion from Caernarfon involves taking the Sherpa Bus to the base of Mount Snowdon (the highest peak in Wales), where you can walk up to the peak on one trail and down another. The climb is difficult, but the views are priceless. However, this ascent is no secret, and you will not be alone on this superhighway to the sky. You may also take the steam train (tel. 01286-870223) from Llanberis and other points along the way to the summit, walk down along any of the trails, and wait for the Sherpa Bus to arrive. (Information at any local tourist office or write to National Park Office, Penrhyndeudraeth, Gwynedd LL48 6LS—include a self-addressed 6x9 envelope.)

Walk 18: Central Wales

Walk: **Chirk to Llangollen via the Shropshire Union Canal/Offa's Dyke**

160 mins.
7.5 miles (12 km)

General Description

Chirk is a pleasantly anonymous town whose fame claim is its eponymous castle. Chirk Castle is unique in that it has been inhabited since its construction almost 700 years ago. Elegant in its inhabited luxury, this fortress contains some of the most striking public rooms in Wales. A visit is worthwhile, but unless you wish to extend your walk by three miles (4.8 km) it is better visited before or after your arrival at Llangollen.

The long (circa $\frac{1}{4}$-mile) tunnel that marks the beginning of the trail was used for canal barges during the nineteenth century. Although nautical traffic through the tunnel is now mechanized, the towpath still exists and offers a fascinating walk back to a simpler, non-mechanized period of time. However, if you have claustrophobia or dislike the idea of not being able to see your feet as you walk in the darkness (the path is perfectly safe with a rail to protect you from tumbling into the murky waters and there is always light on both sides of the tunnel), you may wish to start at the train station. Emerging from the stygian darkness of the tunnel, you will enter a shimmering, emerald-hued valley quietly tucked away from the stress of the twentieth century. Frolicking ducks float in the serene but rather murky water. However, even in such a pacific environment, you are not completely safe from mass media: informative billboards designed to lure portly boaters to food and beverages dot certain segments of this trail. For example, you will observe a sign indicating "Watering Hole Bar and Restaurant Open Seven Days a Week." Unfortunately, unless you enjoy swimming across canals, these watering holes are inaccessible to walkers. A sign on the second tunnel indicates that a taxi is accessible at 773480. There is, however, no phone visible.

When you arrive at well-appointed Froncystyllte, refreshments are available on the main street which parallels the trail. Just beyond Froncystyllte you will cross a towering and lengthy viaduct; the panoramic vistas of the surrounding countryside are astonishing. Beyond the viaduct, the towpath remains level but the surrounding terrain becomes quite hilly, offering excellent views of grazing beasts and thick forest. As barge traffic thickens near Llangollen you will quickly saunter past a flotilla of torpid vessels even while maintaining an easy pace. Resist the urge to admonish indolent boat potatoes to get out and walk the rest of the way.

Diminutive but winsome Llangollen serves as the site of the International Eisteddfod, an international song festival during the early part of July. During this period, accomodations are virtually impossible to obtain; however, during other times of the year rooms are usually available. Throughout the year, Llangollen also serves as a center for outdoor activities, particularly boating and canoeing. If you are not fatigued upon arrival in Llangollen take the strenuous but short hike up to the twelfth-century Dinas Bran fortress, which dominates the town from its lofty perch; otherwise stroll along the commercial streets listening to Welsh being spoken at a rapid clip or relax at a café in this welcoming municipality.

Optional Maps: Landranger 126, 117/Pathfinder 806, 827

Time/Distance: 2 hours 40 minutes/7.5 miles (12 km) (plus 3 miles/ 5 km for optional castle visit)

Difficulties: None

Toilet Facilities: Chirk, Llangollen, Froncystyllte; some privacy

Refreshments: Chirk, Llangollen, Froncystyllte

Getting There: Four to six buses run from Llangollen to Chirk daily. Schedules are available at the Castle Street tourist office in Llangollen. You have three options for starting this walk: 1. Have the driver drop you in town, visit the town, and walk out to the train station; 2. Have the driver drop you at the train station; 3. Continue on the bus beyond the station in order to include the Chirk tunnel in your walk.

Trail Notes

___ 1a. If you start at the tunnel, the bus will drop you at a dead end in the road. As you face the long viaduct, you will see a trail leading down to you left which you will take. When you get to the bottom go right and through the tunnel.

___ 1b. If you start at the train station, you will find the canal just beyond the tracks. Turn right along the tracks.

___ 1c. If you start at the town, walk to the train station (there are signs) and follow the above directions.

___ 1d. From any of the above points, simply follow the canal towpath. You cannot become lost.

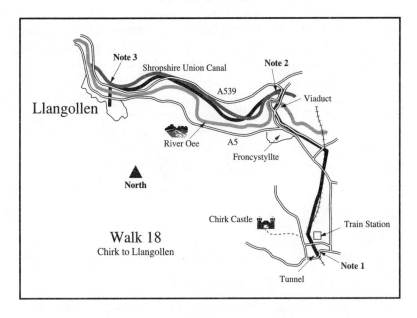

Note 3
Shropshire Union Canal
Note 2
A539
Viaduct
Llangollen
River Oee
A5
Froncystyllte
North
Chirk Castle
Train Station
Walk 18
Chirk to Llangollen
Note 1
Tunnel

___ 2a. Just beyond the viaduct at Froncystyllte, you will see a sign leading you left to Llangollen along the canal.

___ 2b. In a few minutes you will come to a small bridge which you will cross to the other side of the canal where you will continue along the towpath to Llangollen.

___ 3. At the first bridge, turn left into Llangollen.

Suggestions for More Walking

This nineteenth-century towpath provides a tranquil respite from twentieth-century chaos. Just beyond the tunnel, a sign directs you to Chirk Castle, which is a three-mile round trip. Unless you have a long walking day planned or do not have a car, it is probably better to visit the castle later by car. From Llangollen, it is a four-mile (6.4 km) round trip to the remains of the twelfth-century Valle Crucis Abbey north of the town. The route is clearly delineated on Pathfinder map 806. It is possible to either follow route A539 or the course of the Llangollen Railway (tel. (01978-

860951) until you reach the trail. Also, you may take the Llangollen Railway steam train to a variety of stops and walk back along the towpath which parallels the tracks to Llangollen.

Walk 19: Ironbridge

Walk: **Buildwas Abbey to Ironbridge**

General Description

45 mins.
2.2 miles (3.5 km)

Today's time trek begins in the remote medieval past and, within a couple of miles, passes to the dawn of the modern age. All of this takes place within the sobering shadow of a nuclear power plant, emphasizing our remoteness from not only the Middle Ages but also from the last century.

Buildwas Abbey, constructed during the twelfth century, sits quietly along the banks of the River Severn. Never a contender for great size or fame (its primary and limited source of income was derived from bridge tolls), Cistercian Buildwas carried out its 400-year career in distinguished obscurity. Today, as you wander about the well-groomed ruins, you will not be disturbed by crowds of tourists; instead, you will internalize the lonely serenity (occasionally punctuated by Welsh marauders from the West) that characterized much of medieval England.

As you complete the quick ramble alongside the River Severn, scurrying past a group of imposing nuclear silos, reflect on the transitory nature of what we think are permanent states of affairs. The medieval mind did not anticipate the birth of the Industrial Revolution at Ironbridge; the early modern mind did not predict the rise of the Nuclear Age; and we, especially with the accelerated pace of history, do not know what events will soon take precedence in world affairs.

Ironbridge is often called the "birthplace of the Industrial Revolution." The experiments performed here by Abraham Darby revo-

lutionized the iron industry, making it possible for iron to be used for wheels, rails, steam engines, locomotives, ships, and Ironbridge's eponymous iron bridge (the world's first, built in 1776). The town, its appearance scarcely changed from the eighteenth century, functions as a beautifully situated open-air museum. The magnificent Iron Bridge still stands as a monument to Abraham Darby's foresight; cross the bridge and visit the tollhouse which is now an information center with displays illustrating the bridge's history. Touring the Ironbridge complex of museums can easily take a full day. To aid your visit, a shuttle bus commutes regularly among all of the major sites. The do-not-miss attractions include Blists Hill Open Air Museum, a 50-acre re-creation of a late nineteenth-century community; the Museum of Iron, which houses an amazingly engrossing history of iron and its uses; and the Darby Furnace, where Abraham Darby's experiments changed forever the course of world history. Also worthy of a stop is the Museum of the River and Visitor Center, a restored wharf and warehouse providing an audio-visual introduction to the area. Die-hard museum devotees will also want to visit the Jackfield Tile Museum and the Coalport China Museum. Attention troglodytes: do not miss the Tar Tunnel and its natural flowing bitumen. The Ironbridge Gorge Museum Passport, available at any museum, will allow you to visit all of these sites for a single reasonable price.

Optional Maps: Landranger 127/Pathfinder 890

Time/Distance: 45 minutes/2.2 miles (3.5 km)

Difficulties: None

Toilet Facilities: Buildwas Abbey, Ironbridge

Refreshments: Buildwas Abbey, Ironbridge

Getting There: From Ironbridge, take the Wrekin Rambler bus #X96 (Williamson's Motorways, tel. 01743-231010, schedules also at the Ironbridge tourist office), which runs approximately every two hours, to the junction of A4169 and B4380. Ask the driver to let you off at the road that leads to Buildwas Abbey.

Trail Notes

__ 1.   You will exit the bus at a bridge over the River Severn. Cross the bridge, walk along A4169, and turn right at the first road which leads to Buildwas Abbey (you will see a sign).

__ 2a. After you visit the abbey, walk back over the bridge where the bus dropped you and turn right on the road (B4380) which leads back to Ironbridge.

__ 2b. As you walk along the road, look to your right for a path that will soon take you down to the River Severn. Follow this path along the river back to Ironbridge.

__ 3. About midway into the walk, the path will force you to ascend to the road. Walk along the road for a short while looking to your right for a path that will take you down to the river again.

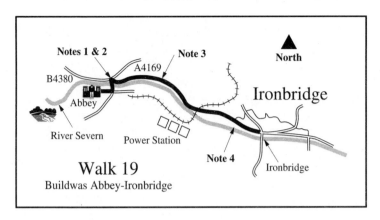

Walk 19
Buildwas Abbey-Ironbridge

___ 4. When you reach Ironbridge, the path will force you up to the road by the museum. Turn right, and you will soon be at the Iron Bridge

Suggestions for More Walking

There is no official name for the path that connects Buildwas Abbey with Ironbridge and no suitable method for expanding this walk in either direction. There are, however, a variety of rural rights of way in the surrounding area. Unfortunately, they are not marked, but if you are looking for some adventure, purchase Pathfinder map 890 and head out on one of these attractive rural trails. You cannot become too far separated from roads and civilization.

Walk 20: Wales/Pembrokeshire Coast

Walk: Solva to St. David's via the Pembrokeshire Coast Path

General Description

**105 mins.
5 miles (8 km)**

Solva's harbor lies tranquilly along an inlet scarcely visible from the Atlantic Ocean and therefore often unnoticed by less-than-wary pirates searching for plunder. At one time Solva was a bustling international seaport where prospective Americans could purchase a passage to the New World for about £4. No longer a port of any significance, Solva rests sleepily but picturesquely as a recreational center and a fine place to embark on foot over a scenic trail.

The trail skirts the harbor, ascends steeply, and quickly reaches the sheer cliffs that you will follow into St. David's. This is an exhilarating adventure in which you will survey some of Britain's most stunning coastal scenery. Wind, waves, and sea gulls will be your constant companions—a wonderfully wild afternoon.

St. David's is a destination worthy of the walk that precedes it. This elfin city, home of a magnificent cathedral, enchants visitors with its peninsular loneliness. Although the cathedral and associated Bishop's Palace form the nucleus of Britain's smallest settlement to be given the status of city, there are numerous other sites in and around St. David's that will hold your interest and make your journey here worthwhile. The tourist office has an excellent brochure "A Quick Look at St. David's," which outlines a walking tour of 37 local sites.

Optional Maps: Landranger 157/Pathfinder 1055

Time/Distance: 1 hour 45 minutes/5 miles (8 km)

Difficulties: Some minor climbs

Toilet Facilities: Solva, St. David's; some privacy

Refreshments: Solva, St. David's

Getting There: From St. David's New Street, take the bus (#340) to Solva. Buses run every 45–60 minutes.

Trail Notes

___ 1a. From the bus stop at Solva (ask to exit at the harbor), walk back to the parking lot and continue to the end of the parking lot (do not cross to the other side of water).

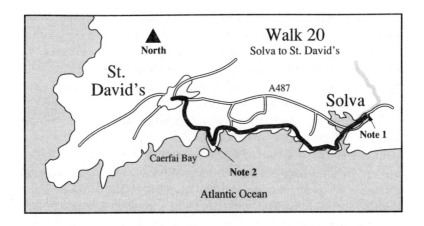

Walk 20
Solva to St. David's

___ 1b. At the end of the parking lot, you will see an asphalt path that eventually goes up.

___ 1c. At the first fork, go right and up the stairs (you will have already seen the first trail maker). You will pass through a gate at the top and then a second gate takes you onto the coastal trail. From here until St. David's the trail is easy to follow.

___ 2. Near St. David's (about 90 minutes into the walk) you will come to a large, sandy beach at Caerfai Bay with a nearby caravan park. At this point, the trail crosses a parking lot. Turn right onto the road leading into the parking lot; it goes directly into St. David's (about 15 minutes from the parking lot.

Suggestions for More Walking

This national trail runs for 186 miles (300 km) from Amroth to Dyfed. Skirting the coast along cliffs, beaches, and dunes throughout its entire length, this trail is peerless for its rugged beauty. John Merrill's *Walking the Pembrokeshire Coast*, JNM Publications, 1992, describes the course of the trail. The tourist office at St. David's has information about circular walks from St. Davids and other points in the area.

Walk 21: Wales/Wye Valley

Walk: **Tintern Abbey to Chepstow Castle via the Wye Valley Walk**

135 mins.
5.5 miles (8.8 km)

General Description

The Wye is well-known as one of Britain's most beautiful river valleys. The trek today, between two of Wales's most famous sites and along an enchantingly beautiful trail, will rouse accolades and result in fine memories. Wordsworth, accompanied by the muses, wandered through the Wye region and found the poetic inspiration here for his "Lines Written Above Tintern Abbey."

The abbey's impressive ruins, surrounded by gently-sloping green hills and enveloped in a pristine valley, stand defiantly against time and virtually untouched by the twentieth century. The ruins date primarily from the thirteenth century and typify the Cistercian desire for simplicity. You will linger long among these ruins that followers of the nineteenth-century Romantic movement found irresistable and commune with their spirits, finding mystery and romance among the silent stones.

Leaving the abbey, the path plunges you, almost immediately, into the enshrouding depths of a shimmering, green forest. Distant views reward your climb from the abbey while dense stands of timber protect you from strong winds blowing over the Welsh hills. Approaching Chepstow, the River Wye becomes increasingly more visible as its winds along an often intricate path to its final destination, the Atlantic Ocean. Outstanding and private views of Chepstow Castle, the town, and the massive suspension bridge greet you as you make your final approach to Chepstow.

Chepstow Castle, today's terminus, looms impressively on its cliff-top perch over the River Wye. Begun in the eleventh century by an associate of William the Conqueror, it was a stronghold on the western march of the newly vanquished Norman territories.

Tour the walls and enjoy the related exhibits within the stronghold—Chepstow Castle will transport you through time and into the remote medieval past. The partially-walled town is quite attractive and serves as a comfortable overnight stop.

Optional Maps: Landranger 162/Outdoor Leisure Map 14

Time/Distance: 2 hours 15 minutes/5.5 miles (8.8 km)

Difficulties: 25-minute climb out of Tintern and frequent minor ups and downs

Toilet Facilities: Tintern Abbey, Chepstow; much privacy

Refreshments: Tintern Abbey, Chepstow

Getting There: From Chepstow take the Red and White Bus #69 to Tintern (tel. Chepstow 622947). Ask the driver to drop you at the abbey.

Trail Notes

___ 1a. After you visit the abbey, walk back to the bus stop. You will see a sign indicating the Wye Valley Walk. The path goes to your right and up.

___ 1b. When the path begins to curve, go left (an arrow points in both directions, but left takes you back to Chepstow).

___ 1c. Continue straight on the broad path, ignoring the footpath sign indicating "Black Cliff." After climbing for about fifteen minutes, you will see a Wye Valley sign marker: follow it up some stairs to your left.

___ 2. When you come to a clearing, look across to a wooden utility pole which has a trail marker affixed. You will enter another section of forest where another arrow puts you on the correct path. Watch for the yellow blazes painted on trees in this section of the woods.

___ 3. About 40 minutes into the walk, the trail hits a dead end at another trail. A right turn is well marked.

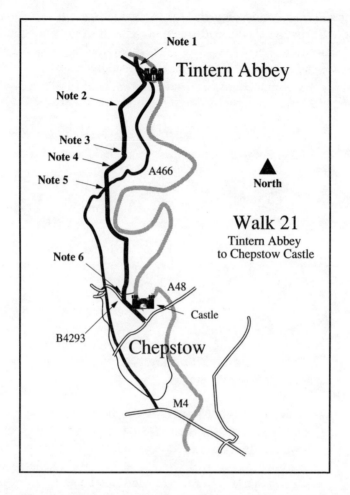

Note 1

Tintern Abbey

Note 2

Note 3
Note 4

A466

Note 5

▲
North

Walk 21
Tintern Abbey
to Chepstow Castle

Note 6

A48

Castle

B4293

Chepstow

M4

___ 4a. About 53 minutes into the walk you will come to a point where there is a panoramic look-out with benches and distant views of Chepstow. Go to the left after you have departed the viewing area.

___ 4b. A couple of minutes later you will come to a small clearing where there are benches; turn left, you will soon see a trail marker.

___ 5a. When you reach the road (A466), cross to the other side. You will see a map of the general area; from this point walk right to the end of the parking lot where you will see an arrow leading you back into the woods.

___ 5b. From this point, stay on the path; it is not always well marked but you will not get lost since there is nowhere else to go.

___ 6. When you finally reach a road (B4293), turn left and you will soon be in Chepstow

Suggestion for More Walking

The Wye Valley Walk follows the serpentine route of the River Wye for 75 miles (121 km) from Haye-on-Wye to Chepstow Castle. A complete description is included in the *Footpath Guide: The Wye Valley Walk Map Pack*, available from the Planning Department, Gwent County Council, County Hall, Cwmbran, Gwent NP44 2XF. This walk is easily extended, since the same bus parallels the trail for about 18 miles (29 km) from Chepstow to Monmouth; for an extra three miles take the bus to the village of Llandrogo.

Walk 22: Oxford

Walk: Radley to Oxford via the Thames River Walk

| 130 mins. |
| 5.5 miles (8.8 km) |

General Description

Oxford, city of dreaming spires, enchants by the antiquity of its elevated, erudite, and edifying ambience. Here in England's oldest college town, one almost expects to see C.S. Lewis lurking intellectually in the deep shadows of a brilliant morning sun. In fact, the magnificent and venerable structures are as beautiful and untainted by progress as they appeared to be in the recent film *Shadowlands*. The streets, however, do not cooperate with the buildings in creating an island of scholarly tranquility—they are constricted with vehicular traffic and its subsequent clamor and pollution. You will need a refreshing pause from the buildings, traffic, and humanity of Oxford, and this trek down the Thames is the highlight of any visit to Oxford.

Today's pilgrimage to the academic mecca of the Western world begins at Radley, a slender, winsome thread of habitations that serves as an upscale bedroom community for Oxfordians in search of quieter quarters. Commuters have built fine homes near the tracks allowing them the luxury of rolling easily into Oxford on public transportation while Jaguars remain tidily tucked in their driveways. Soon out of Radley, you will pass a series of small plots where well-to-do Radlians commune with nature and grow their own vegetables. Leaving the small plots, you will pass through legitimate wheat fields still harrowed by farmers harried by urban encroachment. Fishermen recline lazily along the banks, and pleasure craft ply the placid waters alongside graceful swans. As you approach Oxford, the Thames becomes a playground for athletically inclined academics: walkers, joggers, and cyclists strive for ascendancy along grassy banks while others sail or row through serried waters. There is no better way to participate in the life of the local denizens. The Thames, lined with opulent urban abodes, takes you to the heart of old Oxford, where architectural masterworks and illustrious cityscapes too numerous to mention here serve as a focal point for tourist activity. Detailed guides of Oxford's treasures are available everywhere.

Optional Maps: Landranger 164/Pathfinder 1116

Time/Distance: 2 hours 10 minutes/5.5 miles (8.8 km)

Difficulties: None

Toilet Facilities: Oxford; some privacy

Refreshments: Oxford, pub at Sandford Lock

Getting There: Trains run frequently from Oxford's train station to Radley (numerous buses also pass through Radley).

Trail Notes

___ 1. Radley is a stop with no station. When you exit the train, look back in the direction of Oxford; walk towards the traffic bridge (around 200 yards) that crosses the tracks. When you reach the bridge, turn right onto it, and cross the tracks.

___ 2a. About 10 minutes into the walk, where the road forks, bear left.

___ 2b. About three minutes later, the road ends at a private driveway. Turn left here.

___ 2c. When you reach a point where there is a sign indicating "No Footpath" go right on a trail through the wheat field (there is a yellow arrow pointing the way).

___ 2d. When you reach the Thames, turn left. From this point, the path along the banks is easy to follow into Oxford.

___ 3a. You can enter Oxford's central district, when you reach the Folly Bridge, by turning right.

___ 3b. If you wish to continue directly to the train station, continue past the Folly Bridge along the banks of the Thames. It will appear that you are walking out of town, but you will soon emerge by the train station.

___ 4a. After walking for some distance through a rural area, you will rejoin urbanity along a row of townhouses. You will see a sign "East Street." When this street ends, you will reach a traffic bridge where you turn right and continue to the train station.

___ 4b. When you pass under the train bridge, look left; you will see the train station.

Suggestions for More Walking

The Thames River Walk follows the river's course for 180 miles from Thames Head to London. The entire walk is described in David Sharp's *The Thames Walk*, second edition, Ramblers'

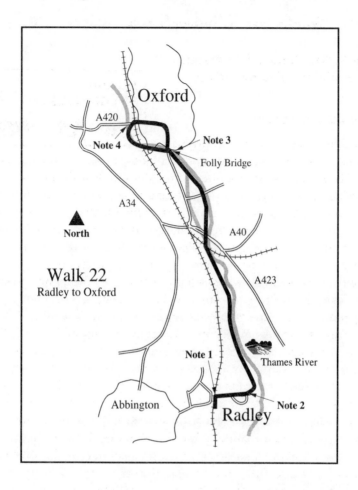

Association, 1990. The above walk can be extended three miles by taking one of the frequent buses from Oxford to Abingdon, home of the very attractive fifteenth-century St. Helen's Church and the remains of a former abbey, and hiking back along the river. Another very attractive alternative involves taking the train north from Oxford to Nethercott and following the towpath of the Oxford Canal seven miles back to Oxford.

Walk 23: Windsor/Eton

Walk: Maidenhead to Windsor/ Eton via the Thames River Walk

140 mins.
6.5 miles (10.5 km)

General Description

Windsor, dominated by the largest in-habited castle in the world, stands majestically along the banks of the River Thames. Main-tourist-attraction Windsor Castle, founded by William the Conqueror in 1070 and now home to Queen Elizabeth several months of the year, is quintessential English pomp and circumstance. Tour buses arrive ad nauseum from London on day trips so you will not be alone as you saunter royally throughout the castle's cavernous interior. In spite of the crowds, the palace is still worth some time, especially if you arrive around opening time just ahead of the throngs of the bus people. Out of the palace and into the streets does not mean you will be huddled with the English masses. Windsor is an upscale community with fine restaurants and shops catering to a most genteel class of society.

Enjoy the refined atmosphere as you walk across the river to Windsor's twin city Eton, home of England's most distinguished boys' school. Founded by Henry VI during the fifteenth century, Eton College still imposes centuries-old traditions on its elite student body, England's future leaders. Wander through the school yard (you may spot a future prime minister), visit the fifteenth-century Lower School, and imbibe at one of the chic cafés along the High Street. Guided tours of the campus are available; inquire at the tourist office.

When you have done the towns, head to Maidenhead where today's trek commences. The initial walk through prosperous Maidenhead takes you directly into the large and elegant shopping district, including a centrally-located indoor mall. Leave your credit cards at the hotel or risk numerous expensive purchases. As you begin to follow the Thames back to Windsor an architectural trove of fabulous homes, mostly late-nineteenth-century and early-twentieth-century with an occasional modern structure thrown in, line the pathway. Some of the estates that you pass have signs like "Warning: Guard dogs loose inside." Avoid the urge to climb over walls in order to verify their presence. In addition to older, classic structures, many new houses are being built along the Thames. If you can afford to live here, you can also skip the trail and float regally upon your yacht into London today.

Beyond Maidenhead, the towpath alternates between clearings and dense foliage. In spite of intense building, there remain, however, great stretches of tranquil uninhabited land. At Boveney, you will pass by the thirteenth-century chapel of St. Mary Magdalene, which stands as a monument to the notion of simplicity-as-beauty. Proximate to Windsor, the bucolic setting is enhanced by youthful rowers from Eton cutting swiftly through the languid waters of the Thames. Finally, the entry into Windsor is perfected by astonishing views of Windsor Castle that reveal its true enormity.

Optional Maps: Landranger 175/Pathfinder 1157, 1173; (the inexpensive A-Z street plan for Slough, Windsor, Maidenhead, and Eton shows the entire route and is quite useful)

Time/Distance: 2 hours 20 minutes/6.5 miles (10.5 km)

Difficulties: None

Toilet Facilities: Maidenhead, Windsor/Eton; some privacy

Refreshments: Maidenhead, Windsor/Eton

Getting There: Take the frequent (every 20 to 40 minutes, schedules available at the Windsor station) 6-minute train ride from Windsor Central Station to Slough where you will transfer to any of the frequent trains that stop at Maidenhead.

Trail Notes

___ 1a. At Maidenhead walk directly ahead from the station, exit to the first street (King Street) and turn left.

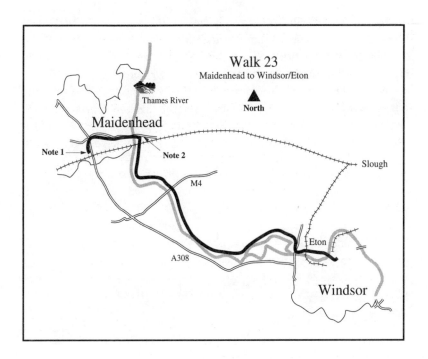

Walk 23
Maidenhead to Windsor/Eton

___ 1b. Continue along King Street until you reach a dead end at High Street, where you turn right.

___ 1c. After about 15 minutes, High Street merges with a main road (Bath Road); continue straight ahead.

___ 2a. When you cross a traffic bridge over the River Thames, turn right at the first road (River Road), a residential road which soon becomes the trail. From this point there is no problem.

___ 2b. Continue along the towpath which takes you directly into Windsor.

Suggestions for More Walking

The Thames River Walk follows the river's course for 180 miles (290 km) from Thames Head to London. The entire walk is described in David Sharp's *The Thames Walk*, second edition, Ramblers' Association, 1990. For another fine walk into Windsor along the Thames, take the train or bus to Staines and hike back the eight miles (13 km) along the towpath. To shorten this walk (to six miles/9.6 km), take the bus to heavily-touristed Runnymede, where King John was forced to sign the Magna Carta by irate nobles in 1215, and walk back along the towpath into Windsor. The only negative associated with this trail is the necessity to walk along B3021 for the last mile into Windsor. The royal family does not want the rabble walking along the towpath within the confines of their property.

Walk 24: Canterbury

Walk: Chilham Castle to Canterbury Cathedral via the North Downs Way/Pilgrims' Way

150 mins.
6 miles (9.6 km)

General Description

Follow an ancient pilgrimage route to one of England's most venerable and bloody cathedrals, site of Thomas à Becket's murder, while dreaming of a lost Chaucerian world. Although the throngs of pilgrims disappeared centuries ago, the trail still winds its merry way to this most hallowed religious shrine. Although slightly out of the way on a short tour of England, Canterbury is worth the detour. The cathedral is peerless as an historical treasure, and the town itself preserves its medieval atmosphere while providing comforting accomodations for the weary traveller. Visit the cathedral; stroll through the the remains of ancient St. Augustine's Abbey; climb to the ruined Norman castle; and linger on the battlements of the fortified West Gate enjoying the panoramic view of the cathedral and surrounding city. The streets and lanes are alive with religious devotees and general merrymakers, and there is always a pub in close proximity.

Today's venture begins at Chilham, a very pleasant ivy-covered town with many ancient homes and a lovely church. The main attraction, however, is the almost unique twelfth-century octoganal castle keep (one of only two remaining in England) surrounded by its award-winning gardens. Next to the castle keep is the seventeenth-century house which has been continuously inhabited to the present day and is open to visitors. The grounds include a 250-acre deer park, a small lake, the Raptor Center, housing an excellent collection of birds of prey, and the award-winning gardens.

Passing alongside the church and then through carefully cultivated fields, you will soon traverse the now-gentrified hamlet of Old Wives Lees, where capacious and carefully-restored country homes (some with thatched rooves) line your route. Departing Old Wives Lees, you enter upon a deeply wooded and tranquil path that gives way to amber wheat fields and expansive orchards as you progress to the next charming village, Chartham Hatch. From this point, the trail ranges through dense forests and an occasional field as it peregrinates to the outskirts of Canterbury and finally through the West Gate and up to the steps of the pilgrim's goal, Canterbury Cathedral.

Optional Maps: Landranger 179/Pathfinder 1211

Time/Distance: 2 hours 30 minutes/6 miles (9.6 km)

Difficulties: Several minor climbs

Toilet Facilities: Chilham, Canterbury; much privacy

Refreshments: Chilham, Chartham Hatch, Canterbury

Getting There: Buses (#400, #401, or #402) run hourly from the Canterbury bus station to Chilham.

Trail Notes

___ 1a. The bus stops in Chilham at Falborough Close. You will see a sign indicating the direction to the castle; continue in that direction to the town's main square.

___ 1b. At the town center, the castle is to your left; to your right is the church. Go right and past the church. You will see the acorn sign indicating the North Downs Way (the Pilgrims' Way corresponds with the North Downs Way on this segment of the trail—you will see signs for both).

___ 1c. Continue along the asphalt road; you will pass two roads in quick succession while continuing straight into Old Wives Lees.

___ 2a. When you come to the grassy traffic island (the only point where several roads intersect) at Old Wives Less, you will see a signpost leading you right.

___ 2b. Continue along this road, looking to your left as you leave the town; turn left at the second asphalt road. You will see a sign that will take you through a gate to your right and onto a deeply wooded path. From here, the trail is adequately marked into Chartham Hatch.

___ 3. Walk into Chartham Hatch until you reach the crossroads where you will see a signpost indicating the direction of the North Downs Way. (Before you reach the crossroads, do not turn left where you see a public footpath sign.)

___ 4a. After crossing a bridge over the expressway (A2), you will turn right and walk along a long hedgerow.

___ 4b. Turn left at the second opening in the hedgerow (it is clearly marked) and continue into Canterbury. (You will not become lost since the first opening also takes you into Canterbury.)

Suggestions for More Walking

The North Downs Way is a national trail that extends for 142 miles (228 km) from Farnham in Surrey to Dover in Kent. Near

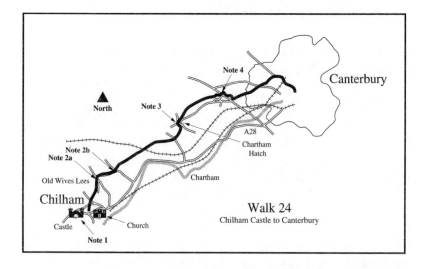

Canterbury, the North Downs Way is often intertwined with the Pilgrims' Way trail. C. J. Wright's *A Guide to the Pilgrims' Way and the North Downs Way*, Constable, 1982, provides a detailed description of both trails. Canterbury's proximity to the sea (about 12 miles/19 km) allows for a day of coastal walking along the Wantsum Walk between Birchington and Herne Bay, both fishing/resort areas. The walk, however, is about twelve miles with no possibility of curtailing its length. Trains run frequently between the towns and the walk, clearly indicated on O.S. Landranger 179, is level and fairly easy.

Walk 25: Eastbourne

Walk: **Beachy Head to East-bourne via the South Downs Way**

General Description

**40 mins.
2 miles (3.2 km)**

A great walk to save for the day before your Gatwick departure from England! The distance from Gatwick is negligible and the walk is short. You could stay at Eastbourne or at one of the airport hotels.

Eastbourne, although slowly fading into obscurity, is still a popular resort and weekend getaway destination for Londoners-on-the-loose looking for breathable air and respite from strident street sounds. During the nineteenth century, Eastbourne was the premier seaside sanctuary for the English upper classes. Fine weather, by English standards, combined with proximity to London, resulted in the explosion of dignified hotels and entertainment complexes worthy of Victorian potentates. The structures remain and are still worthy of a visit, but the upper classes have left for their villas in the south of France. Enjoy the nautical ambience, walk along the extensive seaside promenade among the phantoms of past times, and examine gems from the period of Victorian architecture. Eastbourne will delight, if only for a night.

Beachy Head is the spectacular site of a diminutive lighthouse perched 500 feet above the clamorous sea. The Beachy Head experience is exhilarating, and the short jaunt back to town will leave you with indelible memories of an untamed undulating ocean. Departing Beachy Head, you will be on a well forested, wild flowery path with continuous views of the ocean. Fishing boats bob in the rough surf and sea gulls fly noisily overhead. In less than an hour you will arrive in Eastbourne with plenty of time left to pack or enjoy the town and its delights.

Optional Maps: Landranger 199/Pathfinder 1324

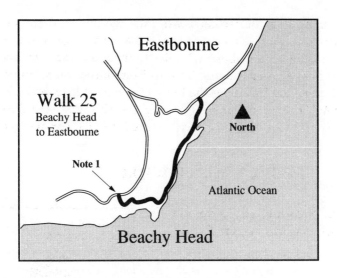

Time/Distance: 40 minutes/2 miles (3.2 km)

Difficulties: None

Toilet Facilities: Beachy Head, Eastbourne

Refreshments: Beachy Head, Eastbourne

Getting There: Take the #3 bus from anywhere along Eastbourne's coastal road to the last stop, Beachy Head.

Trail Notes

___ 1. From the bus stop at Beachy Head walk up the narrow asphalt path until you see the coast where you turn left along the path which is clearly visible all way into Eastbourne.

Suggestions for More Walking

The South Downs Way is a 106-mile-long national trail that commences at Winchester Cathedral and terminates at Eastbourne. For a complete description consult Kev Reynolds' *The South Downs Way and the Downs Link*, Cicerone Press, 1989. If you desire a longer walk along this spectacular coast, take the bus to Eastdene (ask the driver to drop you at the asphalt road that leads to the coast). From Eastdene, it is about 1.2 miles to the coast and then another four miles of coast walking back to Eastbourne. More miles (3.5) could be added by taking the bus to the Exceat Bridge just before entering Seaford and then following the riverside trail down to the ocean. The paths are clearly marked on O.S. Landranger 199.

Walk 26: Isle of Wight

Walk: **Seaview to Ryde via the Isle of Wight Coastal Path**

General Description

70 mins.
3 miles (4.8 km)

Today, you have the opportunity to visit an Atlantic island via a swift ferry, walk a fantastic three oceanside miles, and enjoy the tranquil ambiance of a remarkable seaside resort.

The quick but memorable ferry ride offers outstanding views of both the Isle of Wight and Portsmouth. After a rapid rail ride along a long dock to Ryde you will arrive at a destination steadily growing in popularity. Long the preserve of yachtsmen, the Isle of Wight has become increasingly attractive to a variety of less-than-patrician types, including walkers. If you cannot yacht your way around the island, walk though the landscape that has been called "England in miniature." This small island mimics not only the coastal beauty of its big sister but also the wonderfully varied terrain of the interior. An entire vacation could be spent here.

The aptly named Seaview, with its easy-going harbor life, is a picturesque and pacific village worthy of a lunch pause or an extended delay at a beach-front café lingering over your favorite libation. The short jaunt from Seaview to Ryde follows the ocean along deep, sandy beaches. The views into the ocean are often remarkable. As you enter Ryde, the promenade is teeming with visitors enjoying the balmy weather of England's deepest south. Ryde is renowned for its fabulous Victorian buildings, and a quick stroll through the town will delight devotees of nineteenth-century architecture. Stay for dinner, fresh seafood perhaps, or pass the night in this small gem of a city. A cruise to the Isle of Wight is time well spent.

Optional Maps: Landranger 196/Outdoor Leisure 29

Time/Distance: 1 hour 10 minutes/3 miles (4.8 km)

Difficulties: None

Toilet Facilities: Seaview, Ryde

Refreshments: Numerous opportunities along the route

Getting There: From Portsmouth, ferries depart for Ryde every thirty to sixty minutes. From the ferry station at Ryde, there is a small free shuttle into the town. Exit at the first stop which is at the bus station. Buses (#12) run frequently from Ryde to Seaview, and the schedule is prominently posted at the bus station. Long-distance walkers will particularly enjoy the numerous overnight and dining possibilities that the Isle of Wight offers.

Trail Notes

___ 1. At Seaview, simply walk to the beach and turn left at the concrete path. Follow the oceanside path into Ryde. You cannot become lost.

Suggestions for More Walking

Almost 70 miles in circumference, the Isle of Wight Coastal Footpath completely encircles this pleasant island. John Merrill's *Isle of Wight Coast Path*, JNM Publications, 1988, provides a complete description. Buses parallel many sections of the trail, particularly in the east and south of the island, making it easy to select from numerous segments of this enchanting pathway. Consult O.S.

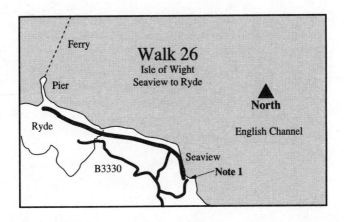

Walk 26
Isle of Wight
Seaview to Ryde

Outdoor Leisure map 29 for a suitable segment and consult bus schedules at Ryde.

Walk 27: Winchester

Walk: Shawford to Winchester via the Itchen Way

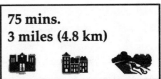

75 mins.
3 miles (4.8 km)

General Description

Today's walk takes you down a remote rural river, up an ancient fortified hill, and into famous Winchester Cathedral.

Winchester's hallowed past includes many moments of glory. Habitation is this area is quite ancient, and a variety of Iron Age remnants have been uncovered. Winchester, itself, has long been an important center of religion and politics: capital of not only Alfred the Great but also William the Conqueror whose underlings compiled the Domesday Book. It was only after the twelfth century that London began to supersede Winchester as the preferred royal residence. Winchester Cathedral, begun in the late-eleventh century and the longest-standing medieval structure in England, is the city's major attraction. Enjoy a detailed tour of the cathedral interior and the exterior buildings known as the Cathedral Close. Also visit the fourteenth-century Winchester College where you will be able to visit some of the original buildings. The town that developed around these amazing sights retains a charming and amiable atmosphere. Here you may dine well and enjoy the prosperous surroundings often found in the south of England.

Shawford is a shady, typically English village with a hotel, restaurant, post office, and a few shops—an excellent place to stop for a lazy lunch or drink before walking back to bustling Winchester. You will follow the Itchen, a slow moving, shallow sliver of a river whose fauna encroaches from all directions threatening a leafy strangulation. The path itself, often shaded by overhanging foliage and accompanied by numerous species of wildflower, seems to float along an emerald green mirage. To your left, country estates, mostly from the twentieth century, line the river banks.

About fifteen minutes out of Shawford, the trail passes through pastures teeming with grazing beasts; soon you will arrive at St. Catherine's Hill. At one time this hill was fortified; although no walls are currently standing, the foundations are clearly visible around the hill's perimeter. The strenuous walk to the top provides you with an excellent example of the difficulty our ancestors had surviving in a hostile world, and the views of Winchester and the Itchen Valley from St. Catherine's Hill are stunning. The walk from St. Catherine's Hill into Winchester takes you quickly from the remote Iron Age past, through medieval quarters, and into the twentieth century.

Optional Maps: Landranger 185/Pathfinder 1264

Time/Distance: 1 hour 15 minutes/3 miles (plus 20 minutes for the St. Catherine's Hill excursion)

Difficulties: None

Toilet Facilities: Shawford, Winchester

Refreshments: Shawford, Winchester

Getting There: Trains run every 20 to 60 minutes from Winchester to Shawford. Be certain to ride on one of the front cars—the platform at Shawford is short, meaning it is impossible to exit from the rear cars.

Trail Notes

___ 1a. When you exit from the train at Shawford, walk through the tunnel to the other side of the tracks where you come to a road.

___ 1b. When you come to the road, go to your right; you will see a bridge directly ahead and the Bridge Hotel. Continue along the road, cross over the bridge, and you will see the footpath sign where you will go left along the River Itchen.

___ 2. After about forty minutes, you will come to a tunnel (to your right) that goes under a road that the trail parallels. Turn right here if you wish to visit St. Catherine's Hill.

___ 3. After leaving St. Catherine's Hill and returning to the trail, you will come to a small bridge. Here you can either follow the way indicated by the footpath, or look to your left where you will see the river and follow the riverside path into town. Both take you to the same place, but the riverside path is more scenic. (There is a sign indicating "No Public Access," but it is a public right of way for walkers; you have every right to follow this path into the city.)

___ 4. When you reach Winchester, and are no longer able to follow the river, you will begin to see signs that lead you to the cathedral and High Street. From High Street, signs will direct you to the railway station.

Suggestions for More Walking

There is no official guide to the Itchen Way, which extends about twelve miles (20 km) along the River Itchen and the Itchen

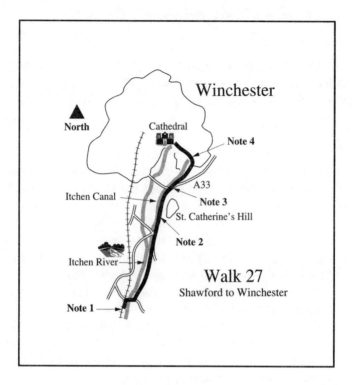

Navigation Canal from Southampton on the coast to just beyond Winchester. The trail is usually easy to follow and the above walk can be extended by exiting either at Eastleigh or Swaything. Be certain to purchase the O.S. Pathfinder maps 1264 and 1284, which clearly show the trail and your route from the train stations to the trail.

Walk 28: Stonehenge/Salisbury

Walk: Stonehenge to Salisbury (Old Sarum) via the Wessex Way and the Wiltshire Cycle Way

180 mins.
7.5 miles (12 km)

General Description

Stonehenge is one of Britain's premier tourist attractions. Mysterious megaliths still astonish and bewilder modern pilgrims who do not readily accept the assertion that the stones were transported from Ireland by Merlin's magical powers or erected by an extinct race of giants. With obvious religious intent, Stonehenge was sedulously elevated over several centuries until it reached its present form around 1500 BC. The technology used to transport and raise these massive blocks of stone still provokes competing theories, but everyone agrees that their elevation was phenomenally advanced for Bronze Age Britain. This is not an attraction that will take several hours of intense touring; a quick walk around the periphery and, perhaps, a meditative interlude of reverent astonishment will suffice. Even after a short viewing, the images will long remain vividly etched in your mind.

Departing Stonehenge and other tourists, you will enter a pleasant, rolling land that offers excellent vistas in all directions of the Salisbury Plain's great expanse. As you traverse amber waves of grain and fields of grazing sheep, watch for the numerous grassy mounds in the area which were used for burial purposes during the Bronze Age. The River Avon, at this point a fast-moving, swan-laden narrow strip of fluid hidden from most tourists, will be your companion for about half of the walk. Upper Woodford, midway to Old Sarum, offers an excellent pub for lunch or a refreshing beverage. If you are tired, there is a bus stop here where several buses per day return to Salisbury.

Old Sarum, originally an Iron Age hill-fort of Olympian proportions, eventually evolved into the predecessor of contemporary

Salisbury (New Sarum). During the thirteenth century the clergy and people of Old Sarum, no longer needing a defensive mound and facing an indequate supply of water, decided to move the cathedral south to the banks of the River Avon. The present ghost-town withered slowly until it was finally abandoned. The 56 acres of ruins, including remnants of the former cathedral and defensive perimeter, captivate the imagination.

Salisbury's "new" cathedral, completed in 1265, forms the nucleus of the town's medieval quarter. A casual stroll through these aged alleys reveals numerous gabled, half-timbered houses constructed between the fourteenth and seventeenth centuries. The cathedral is one of England's finest, displaying a stylistic unity found in few European cathedrals (a result of its relatively short, four-decade building period). There are also excellent accommodations, restaurants, and shopping opportunities in town, making Salisbury an excellent base for exploring south-central England.

Optional Maps: Landranger 184/Pathfinder 1221, 1241

Time/Distance: 3 hours/7.5 miles (12 km)

Difficulties: Two long but gradual climbs

Toilet Facilities: Stonehenge, Upper Woodford, Salisbury

Refreshments: Stonehenge, Upper Woodford, Salisbury

Getting There: Buses run hourly to Stonehenge from Salisbury's bus station and every 15 minutes back to Salisbury from Old Sarum (schedules at the tourist office or call Wilts and Dorset Buses at 01722-336875 or 01202-673555).

Trail Notes

___ 1a. After visiting Stonehenge, walk back to the road (A344) and turn left.

___ 1b. Follow the road (A344) until you reach the first asphalt road which is called a by-way and is scarcely suitable for vehicular traffic.

___ 1c. Turn left here. Follow this path until you reach the next road (A303) where you turn left and walk until you reach the next gravel road and turn right. Continue straight on this trail.

___ 2. When the trail curves sharply to the left, you will encounter some farm buildings (the only farm buildings that you will encounter up to this point). Before the first building, the trail forks. You will go to the right on a grassy path; do not go straight ahead on the gravel path.

___ 3a. After about 55 minutes, the trail turns sharply left. At this point, look to your left as you continue along the trail; when you see a gravel road going uphill turn right along the field following the path into the forest straight ahead.

___ 3b. About twenty feet into the forest, there is a clearly defined path where you will turn left.

___ 4. As you leave the forest, you will cross an asphalt road

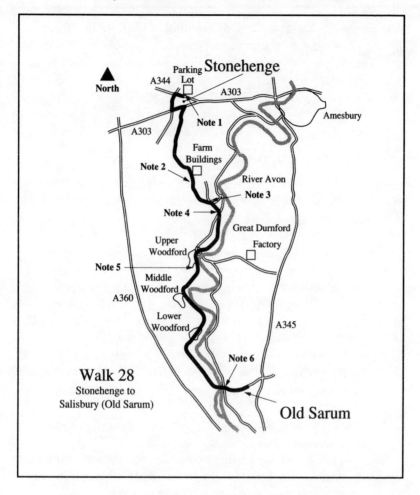

North

Stonehenge

Parking Lot

A344

A303

Amesbury

Note 1

A303

Farm Buildings

Note 2

River Avon

Note 3

Note 4

Great Durnford

Upper Woodford

Factory

Note 5

Middle Woodford

A360

Lower Woodford

A345

Note 6

Walk 28
Stonehenge to
Salisbury (Old Sarum)

Old Sarum

and see a sign indicating "Bridal Path to Gt. Durnford." Follow this path to your right and continue into Upper Woodford. Do not cross the bridge over the River Avon into Great Durnford unless you wish to visit this picturesque town.

___ 5a. When you reach an asphalt road, go left. You are in Upper Woodford, a good place to stop for lunch.

___ 5b. From Upper Woodford simply continue along the seldom-travelled asphalt road (known as the Wiltshire Cycle Way) through Middle and Lower Woodford until you reach Old Sarum.

___ 6. When the road crosses the River Avon and reaches a dead end at another asphalt road, turn left and then quickly right onto another asphalt road that will take you to Old Sarum.

Suggestions for More Walking

The Wessex Way extends 104 miles (167 km) from Marlborough to Swanage on England's south coast. For a complete description, consult Alan Proctor's *The Wessex Way*, Thornhill Press, 1980. Public transportation and interesting trails do not seem to often connect in the Salisbury Plain. It is better to simply move on to the next major area rather than look in vain for another suitable walk in the vicinity of Salisbury.

Walk 29: Weymouth/Chesil Beach

Walk: Portland Bill to Chesil via the Southwest Coastal Path

80 mins.
3.2 miles (5.1 km)

General Description

Weymouth is one of the few English seaside resorts that still attracts throngs of visitors, and the weather is usually good by English standards. Since the eighteenth century Weymouth has been renowned for its fine sandy beaches and attractive harbor area that are its main attractions. If you find a room (the tourist office usually has some vacancies), you may be quite content to relax here for a few days while lying on the beach and imbibing the nautical ambiance.

Portland Bill is the southern tip of the Isle of Portland where a lonely (except for the day tourists) lighthouse guides sailors away from lofty cliffs. Climb to the top for astonishing views, stop at

the proximate café, and quickly embark upon the trail. Five minutes away from the lighthouse, you will begin a memorable walk along sheer cliffs with immense views of the Atlantic Ocean and sandy beaches far below. The crowds are left far behind.

Chesil, the terminus of this walk, functions as a quieter place of sojourn to the bustle of Weymouth. Situated astride the miles-long Chesil Beach, it has all the necessary amenities and accommodations for a quick lunch or a summer stay.

Optional Maps: Landranger 194/Pathfinder 1343 (also the A-Z city map of Weymouth includes a highly detailed map of the Isle of Portland)

Time/Distance: 1 hour 20 minutes/3.2 miles (5.1 km)

Difficulties: None

Toilet Facilities: Portland Bill, Fortuneswell

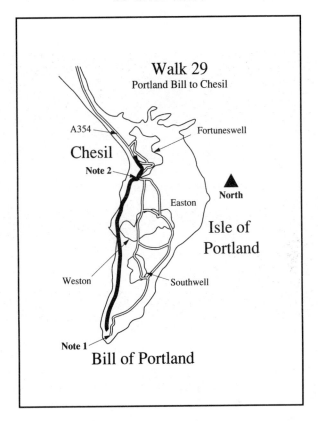

Walk 29
Portland Bill to Chesil

A354

Fortuneswell

Chesil

Note 2

North

Easton

Isle of Portland

Weston

Southwell

Note 1

Bill of Portland

Refreshments: Portland Bill, Fortuneswell

Getting There: Buses run from Weymouth to Portland Bill every twenty to sixty minutes. If you have a car, you may wish to drive to Fortuneswell and catch the bus there, which eliminates the need to take the bus to Weymouth.

Trail Notes

___ 1. The trail begins at the northwest corner of the parking lot at Portland Bill right next to a military installation. Continue north; you cannot become lost.

___ 2. When you reach the first vehicular road (New Road) walk along it looking to your left. You will soon see a set of stairs that will take you down to Chesil beach, where you will encounter a bus stop at the bottom.

Suggestions for More Walking

The Southwest Coastal Path rambles 594 miles (956 km) along the Atlantic coast from Minehead on the northern coast of the Cornwall peninsula to Poole, west of Weymouth. Martin Collins' two-volume *The South West Way: A Walker's Guide to the Coastal Path*, Cicerone Press, 1989, provides a complete description of the trail. For a longer walk, take the bus to Abbotsbury and walk back about nine miles to Weymouth via the Southwest Coastal Path. The trail ranges through the interior until it reaches the coast of the lagoon formed by Chesil beach.

Walk 30: Cornwall Peninsula

Walk: Land's End to St. Just via the Southwest Coastal Path

160 mins.
6.5 miles (10.5 km)

General Description

The appropriately named Land's End marks England's western extremity. Unfortunately, there is no end-of-the-world loneliness awaiting the visitor. This promontory of ethereal beauty has been shamelessly co-opted by a garish amusement park and throngs of its corpulent patrons. Still, the voyage here is worthwhile, and the views stunning. Furthermore, ten minutes beyond the hysteria of Land's End you will be often by yourself on equally alluring terrain.

Not far beyond Land's End lies Sennen Cove, a diminutive and pleasant locale suitable for a relaxing sojourn—a broad, lengthy beach and unhurried atmosphere being its main attractions. Here, according to legend, King Arthur and the combined armies of seven Cornish kings defeated a horde of blood-thirsty Danish invaders. Beyond Sennen Cove, the trail continues to traverse lofty cliffs, rocky coves, and wide sandy beaches. The grassy slopes towering over the beaches are ablaze with purple and yellow wildflowers; numerous species of birds ply the air emitting a cacophony of tones that clash strikingly with the crashing of waves on rock. There is a savage majesty about this trail found nowhere else in England. Granite-built trails-end St. Just welcomes the cliff hiker with a number of fine pubs and restaurants—a drink or meal being requisite for processing the experience of the preceding magnificence.

There are accommodations in Land's End and Sennen Cove; however, if you prefer a larger locale try closely proximate, piratical Penzance. You will believe that pirates did at one time live here.

Optional Maps: Landranger 203/Pathfinder 1364, 1368

Time/Distance: 2 hours 40 minutes/6.5 miles (10.5 km)

Difficulties: Frequent minor climbs, some rather strenuous

Toilet Facilities: Land's End, Sennen Cove, St. Just

Refreshments: Land's End, Sennen Cove, St. Just

Getting There: From the St. Just bus station, one bus (Western National, tel. Penzance 01736-69469) in the late morning and one bus in the afternoon go to Land's End (except Saturdays). If you are staying in Penzance and do not have a car, numerous buses go between the Penzance bus station and St. Just.

Trail Notes

___ 1a. The bus stops at Land's End's parking lot. Walk through the gates to the exhibits, etc., and continue down to the coast (ignore the admissions information—you are welcome

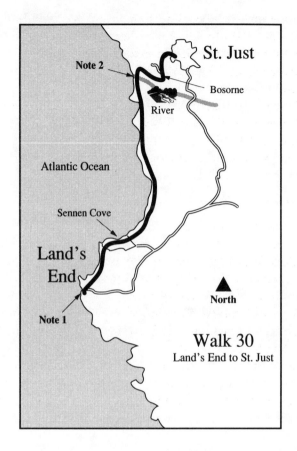

to shop, use the restrooms, and dine in the restaurants without paying admission).

___ 1b. When you reach the coast, turn right and you will soon be on the trail. The trail actually begins just behind a place called the "First and Last Refreshment House." From here the trail is well marked and easy to follow; watch for the yellow arrows and acorn sign.

___ 2a. After about 2 hours and 10 minutes, you will descend from the cliffs at a point where there is a river and a road (the only road you will see beyond Sennen Cove). Cross the river at the small bridge and turn right down the road away from the coast.

___ 2b. Follow the road as it curves until you reach a small cluster of houses called Bosorne. You will see a sign indicating "Cot Valley" pointing in the direction where you have just come from. Turn right here, and you will soon be in St. Just.

Suggestions for More Walking

The Southwest Coastal Path rambles 594 miles (956 km) along the Atlantic coast from Minehead on the northern coast of the Cornwall peninsula to Poole, west of Weymouth. Martin Collins' two-volume *The South West Way: A Walker's Guide to the Coastal Path*, Cicerone Press, 1989, provides a complete description of the trail. For a short cliff-top excursion, simply walk the 1.6 miles from Land's End to Sennen Cove (you may leave your car at Sennen Cove and take the bus to Land's End or buses return from Sennen Cove to Penzance or St. Just). Purchase J. R. Nicholls' inexpensive booklet *Six Coastal Walks with Inland Returns in Penwith* at many local stores and tourist offices for some additional coastal walking.

Walk 31: Glastonbury

Walk: Over the Tor and into Glastonbury via the Somerset Way

35 mins.
1.4 miles (2.2 km)

General Description

Glastonbury is the tie-dye capital of England, a mecca for "New Age Travellers" (they look like hippies from Haight-Ashbury during the sixties). This is a town where formal attire means black and white tie-dye, and youthful travellers vagabond throughout the area in Mad Max assemblages of vehicles. Merlin himself in full magician's regalia could stroll city streets unnoticed.

Glastonbury's attraction for the mystically inclined is its associations with the Arthurian legend and Christianity. According to tradition King Arthur is buried in Glastonbury Abbey; Glastonbury Tor (the remains of St. Michael's Chapel on a steep hill) is the site of the Isle of Avalon; and the Chalice Well is the location of the Holy Grail. Jesus supposedly accompanied Joseph of Arimathea to Glastonbury, and Joseph, after Jesus' death, returned to build England's first Christian church on the site of the abbey. It is also claimed that the remains of Ireland's St. Patrick are buried here, and St. George slew the dragon in the general vicinity.

Today's short but eventful walk over the Tor (Isle of Avalon) takes you past all of the major sites of Glastonbury, and into super-colorful (in a multitude of senses) downtown Glastonbury.

Optional Maps: Landranger 182/Pathfinder 1238

Time/Distance: 35 minutes/1.4 miles (2.2 km)

Difficulties: One strenuous climb

Toilet Facilities: Glastonbury

Refreshments: Glastonbury

Getting There: Take bus marked "Tor" which runs about every twenty minutes throughout the day from near the abbey entrance. Ask the driver to drop you at the far end of the Tor, explaining that you wish to walk back to town.

Trail Notes

___ 1. The trail is clearly marked from the bus stop. Simply ascend along the path.

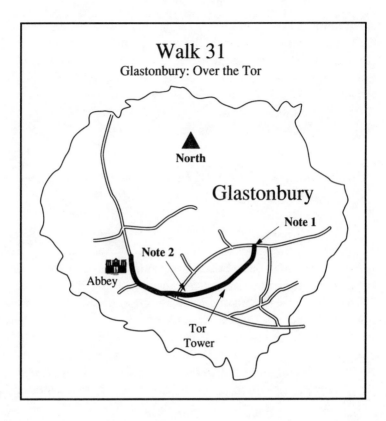

Walk 31

Glastonbury: Over the Tor

North

Glastonbury

Note 1

Note 2

Abbey

Tor
Tower

___ 2. When you have descended from the Tor you will reach a wall; turn left here and then go immediately right on the next road which will take you past the Chalice Well, the Rural Life Museum, and into the center of the town to the Abbey.

Suggestions for More Walking

Combine this short walk with the following walk (Wookey Hole to Wells) for a great day of touring and walking. The Somerset Way extends 108 miles (174 km) from Minehead on the Atlantic Coast to Bath. See Laurence Main's *A Somerset Way*, Thornhill Press, 1980, for a complete description. It is possible to walk from

Glastonbury to Wells via the Somerset Way, but it requires a substantial amount of walking along well-trafficked A39. Other trails
in the area either disappear into farmers' fields, do not have access to public transportation, or require too much road walking.

Walk 32: Wells

Walk: Wookey Hole to Wells via the West Mendip Way

45 mins.
2 miles (3.2 km)

General Description

Wookey Hole (not Chewbacca's birth
place) is a peculiar patina of glossy commercialism veiling places
and articles of genuine interest.

First, line up with bus loads of tourists for a visit to what are
hyped as "Britain's Most Spectacular Caves." Actually the caves
that follow the course of the River Axe and served as a habitation
for early men and women are quite attractive and interesting. Watch
for the legendary witch. Just beyond the caves is Britain's last
handmade paper mill where you can enjoy a demonstration of
this almost lost art. After leaving the paper mill, the rest of the
museum complex, including a Fairground Memories exhibition,
looks like a set from a Fellini film—brilliantly colored and wildly
carved merry-go-rounds, a variety of carnival rides, a mirrored
maze, numerous antique games, etc. The quaint village of the same
name has a hotel, restaurant, Chinese medicine clinic, old church,
and a bakery/tea house.

As you leave the town you walk up a very pleasant grassy path
and into a forest. The challenging climb to the top of the hill is
rewarded by outstanding views of Wells to your right and in the
far distance the Tor at Glastonbury. A moment's pause for quiet
reflection and breath-catching precede a merciful, downhill stroll
along a lovely forested path into Wells.

Wells is one of England's most diminutive but also most attractive cities. The town, characterized by a quiet elegance, stands compactly about its main attraction, the Cathedral Church of St. Andrew. This lovely Gothic structure and its associated buildings, constructed over three centuries, represent one of the most complete cathedral complexes in England. Visit the cathedral, tour the other buildings comprising the complex, and enjoy the comfortable ambience of this pacific patch of urbanity.

Optional Maps: Landranger 182/Pathfinder 1218

Time/Distance: 45 minutes/2 miles (3.2 km)

Difficulties: A strenuous fifteen-minute climb out of Wookey Hole

Toilet Facilities: Wookey Hole, Wells

Refreshments: Wookey Hole, Wells

Getting There: From Wells' Princes Street Bus Station, bus #172 leaves hourly during daylight hours for Wookey Hole (Badgerline, tel. Wells 673084).

Trail Notes

___ 1. From the parking lot where the bus stops, turn right along the road back in the direction of Wells and through the tiny village of Wookey Hole.
___ 2. Follow the road until it curves. You will then see a post with an arrow indicating a footpath that you will turn left onto and follow up to the top of the hill. Follow the fence as you descend. The trail is easy to follow into Wells.
___ 3. At Wells, when the trail reaches a dead end at a wall, turn left and you will soon be in the city center.

Suggestions for More Walking

The West Mendip Way is a scenic, thirty-mile (48 km) swath through Somerset from coastal Weston-super-Mare to Wells Cathedral. A

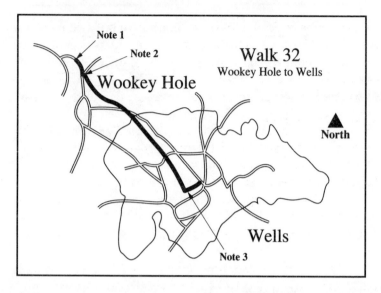

complete description of this trail can be found in Andrew Eddy's *The West Mendip Way*, available from the Weston-super-Mare Civic Society, 3–6 Wadham Street, Weston-super-Mare, Avon BS23 1JY. This walk can be extended to about ten miles by taking the bus from Wells to Cheddar (of cheese fame) and walking back—purchase the West Mendip Way guide and/or O.S. Pathfinder maps 1198 and 1218. Another longer walk (12 miles) would take you from Weston-super-Mare to Cheddar or vice versa. Consult the guide for trail details. Also, there are some circular walks in the area of Wells—inquire at the tourist office.

Walk 33: Bath

Walk: Saltford to Bath via the Avon Walkway

120 mins.
4.8 miles (7.7 km)

General Description

Even before the arrival of the Romans in the first century AD, Bath was known for its warm springs. According to legend, outcast leper Prince Blalud saw his pigs healed of a skin disease after cavorting in the local mud. In a leap of faith, Blalud threw himself into the mud and was healed of his leprosy. The prince was restored to the royal court, fathered the hapless King Lear, and lived happily ever after at Bath.

The Romans established England's first spa resort here, building an extensive system of baths and ancillary structures. The Roman structures were not discovered until the late-nineteenth century when sewer workers happened upon them. Bath's baths are among the best organized and most intriguing tourist sites in England. Tours leave every fifteen minutes through the labyrinthine complex and proceed briskly into Britain's ancient past. Also worthwhile is the city tour, which takes you through Bath's historic center and into the world of eighteenth-century Georgian architecture.

The trail begins at Saltford where you can have a drink, eat a meal, and do some shopping. A nice place but it will not delay you for very long in your quest for the River Avon. Descending to the Avon, you will be greeted by alluring views of this venerable waterway. The path continues into Bath often wedged between the river and alternating fields of golden grain and iridescent displays of wild flowers. Barges and cruisers plod slowly along the tranquil waters while sea gulls and ducks float amiably in their wake. The final approach to Bath is along the Bitton-Bath Cycle Way, which, as an abandoned railway, stands as a sterling example of the possibilities of a more complete rails-to-trails system

in America. This heavily wooded band of shimmering green and wildflowers forms a remarkably serene, nineteenth-century back door into a bustling, twentieth-century metropolis. Entering Bath along the River Avon, you will see ancient factories looming precipitously over the river, massive but long disused freight doors still in evidence. Some have been converted into condos or factories, while others stand abandoned as mute testimony to the temporal distance of the Industrial Revolution.

Optional Maps: Landranger 172/Pathfinder 1183

Time/Distance: 2 hours/4.8 miles (7.7 km)

Difficulties: None

Toilet Facilities: Saltford, Bath

Refreshments: Saltford, Bath

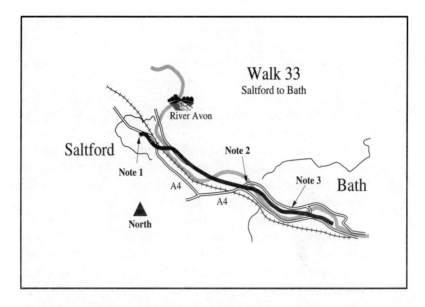

Walk 33
Saltford to Bath

Getting There: From the bus station at Bath (directly across from the train station), take the #339 bus to Saltford (ultimate destination: Bristol). Ask the driver to drop you at the Crown stop (in front of the Crown Hotel in Saltford).

Trail Notes

__ 1a. From the Crown Hotel, walk back down A4 in the direction of Bath.

__ 1b. At the first pedestrian crossing, cross to the other side of the street and turn right (still on A4) continuing downhill in the direction of Bath.

__ 1c. When the road takes a sharp right, you will see a public footpath sign; turn left here and continue along the path.

__ 1d. The path takes you across a short bridge spanning some railway tracks. Turn right on the other side, walking parallel to the tracks, and then quickly left (there is no alternative to the quick left) descending to an asphalt road paralleling the River Avon, where you turn right.

___ 1e. In a couple of minutes, you will turn left at the gate to a public marina where there are numerous boats docked and you may stop for a drink or lunch at the marina restaurant. Walk to the riverside path where you turn right, in the direction of Bath. (The riverside path is a public right of way throughout its length; do not hesitate to climb the occasional gate.)

___ 2a. After about one hour you will go through a short tunnel under a traffic bridge. When you emerge, do not continue along the river. Look across the field; you will see a wooden gate that you should walk towards.

___ 2b. Pass through the gate and walk a few feet up to the asphalt path (formerly a railway bed) which is the Bitton-Bath Cycle Way reserved exclusively for cyclists and pedestrians. This route will take you directly into Bath.

___ 3a. When the cycle way enters the town onto a street, continue straight, looking to your right. Turn right when you see an opportunity to join the riverside path, and continue into the city center.

Suggestions for More Walking

The Avon Walkway follows the Avon River for thirty-one miles (50 km) from Pill (just west of Bristol) to the Dundas Aqueduct, east of Bath. There is no official guide, but an annotated map, *The Avon Walkway*, is available through the Avon County Council, Planning Department, PO Box 46, Avon House North, St. James Barton, Bristol BS99 7EU. This walk can be easily extended by taking the bus or train to Keynsham or even Bristol. For a more remote river-valley walk, take the train to Freshford (one stop south of Bath along the River Avon). Walk south along the tracks until you cross a bridge; look left and go along the first trail, which will take you across the River Avon, then go left along the river and back to Bath (about 7 miles).

Walk 34: Stratford

Walk: Welford-on-Avon to Stratford via the Avon Valley Footpath

105 mins.
5 miles (8 km)

General Description

No city has profited more from the birth of a single citizen. Stratford is a single-industry town: Shakespeare is everywhere. You can visit Shakespeare's birthplace, grammar school, grave, mother's home (four miles north at Wilmcote; see Suggestions for More Walking), and a variety of other Elizabethan sites. Stratford is also home of the Royal Shakespeare Company, considered to be the finest in the world. Shakespeare fans will delight in their fine productions. You will not, however, be alone in Stratford. Tourists overwhelm this living museum and the pace can be frenetic, particularly in the afternoon when tour buses arrive from London. See Shakespearian sites early, go for a stroll through Shakespeare's countryside in the afternoon, and enjoy a world-class Shakespearian production in the evening—a totally satisfying Shakespearian sojourn.

The trail begins at Welford, a small, pleasantly-situated town with a traditional general store, tranquil atmosphere, and picturesque, thatched-roof aspect that appears on the cover of the Landranger map 151. As you leave Welford, the path cuts a swath through large tracts of wheat and quickly arrives at Weston-on-Avon, a super-cute village with white-washed thatched-rooved houses, but no commerce. As you walk along the River Avon, vast fields of wheat are to your right and across the river sheep graze contentedly. An occasional barge or river boat winds its way slowly along the placid waters, and many water lily pads sprout from the shallow waters. This is the land that Shakespeare knew; he would not recognize the city that has grown around his house, but he would recognize the River Avon, the bounteous fields, and the course of today's walk. Allow creative thoughts to permeate your mind.

Optional Maps: Landranger 151/Pathfinder 997

Time/Distance: 1 hour 45 minutes/5 miles (8 km)

Difficulties: None

Toilet Facilities: Stratford

Refreshments: Welford, Weston, Stratford

Getting There: Take the #218 bus to Welford-on-Avon from the bus stop in front of McDonalds on Bridge Street in Stratford. Ask the driver to let you off at the Maypole stop, which is in the center of town. (Buses run hourly; there is a schedule posted at the stop or telephone Stratford Blue at 01788-535555)

Trail Notes

___ 1a. When you descend from the bus, walk back along the road in the direction of Stratford until you reach a sign that indicates "Montague's Corner."

___ 1b. Here where the road curves, look to your right and you will see a sign "Pool Close Footpath." There are two paths here; go right on the one beyond the "Pool Close Footpath" sign which is a gravel road.

___ 2a. In less that ten minutes, you will arrive at Weston-on-Avon and pass through the center of this tiny town.

___ 2b. Continue on the town's asphalt road beyond the church where the road becomes gravel and then a double-track farm road.

___ 3. When this very straight trail makes a noticeable curve to the right, you will see an arrow leading you to the left and down to the River Avon, where you continue along the river banks.

___ 4. About fifty minutes into the walk you will pass over a tiny footbridge. You will see an arrow indicating a sharp right turn on the other side of the fence. Turn right in the field and away from the river while continuing along the

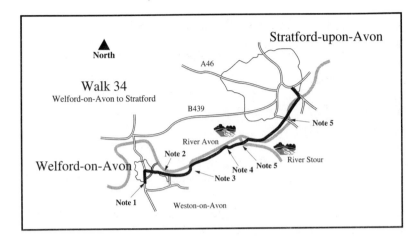

fence until you reach another fence and turn left (you will see an arrow).

___ 5a. The trail leads you to an abandoned rail bridge which is now a cycle route. You will cross two rivers—the River Stour and the River Avon.

___ 5b. When you cross the second river (Avon), descend to your right and continue along the riverside path.

___ 6a. After you pass under the first traffic bridge you will see a pedestrian bridge. Turn right on the pedestrian bridge and cross the river.

___ 6b. When you reach the other side of the river turn left (you will be in a city park) and proceed directly into central Stratford.

Suggestions for More Walking

There is no official guide to the Avon Valley Footpath, but it is clearly marked on the topographical maps and easy to follow. The above walk can be easily extended to a total of ten miles by taking the bus to Bidford-on-Avon and walking back along the Avon. The only drawback is the necessity to walk along the road for about $^2/_3$-mile just beyond Bidford. The trail is clearly marked on the O.S. Pathfinder map 997. For a four-mile jaunt along the towpath of the Stratford-upon-Avon Canal, take the bus to Wilmcote, visit Mary Arden's (Shakespeare's mother) house, and walk back to Stratford. Be certain to have O.S. Pathfinder map 997 and the A-Z street plan of Stratford which will guide you back to your starting point.

Walk 35: Cotswolds

Walk: **Chipping Campden to Broadway via the Cotswold Way**

130 mins.
6 miles (9.6 km)

General Description

Nestled within the rolling green hills of the Cotswolds are some of the most enchanting villages known to humankind. A cruise through these villages is akin to an adventure on a lost plateau—startling remnants of the past stand in striking contrast to modernity, and halcyon days are revived. The ubiquitous and remarkable stone buildings, unique to the villages of this region, have a golden hue similar to that of the setting sun. Stunning stone combined with artful architecture has produced villages of Elysian beauty set in an emerald countryside worthy of Oz. Constructed by wealthy wool merchants, the Cotswold villages owe their remarkably preserved state to the collapse of the wool market and the subsequent obscurity of this region. Currently, the Cotswolds have become popular with tourists; however, there is no over-commercialization, and life still proceeds at a leisurely pace.

Today's rustic route begins with the best £0.80 tour available in England: a slow moving local bus that winds its way along narrow bands of asphalt through a verdant countryside and into quaint villages known only to locals. Descending from the bus, you will begin a trek through often spectacular scenery, rambling between two of the finest villages in one of Britain's most attractive regions.

Chipping Campden was the most prosperous of these towns and this distinction is reflected in the complex of wonderful buildings from numerous periods that blend harmoniously along High Street. The arched and gabled seventeenth-century Market Hall in the town center where the bus stops serves as a focal point for the community. The surrounding merchants offer every sort of convenience, and several excellent restaurants line the streets, making Chipping Campden an excellent base for regional exploration.

As you climb beyond Chipping Campden's last home, the asphalt road becomes dirt and gravel. Pasture and farmland surround; sheep graze contentedly; and the views of Chipping Campden are unparalleled. Still climbing, you will reach Dover's Hill, where the multi-miled views in all directions are stunning and available only to the walker. Coursing along a high ridge you will notice that several benches for tired walkers have been placed along the path. A fine British tradition calls for the placing of a memorial bench in a location that a deceased loved one admired. Watch for the well-situated bench dedicated to Nan Mackay (1909–1971), which is inscribed "Loved This Countryside." Her love was justified. Linger for a while on Nan's bench.

Before your arrival in Broadway pause for a visual feast at the top of Broadway Tower. Built in the late-eighteenth century, during the height of the Romantic period, in the style of a medieval castle keep, its purpose is not completely clear. However, it was probably built as an enhancement to the grounds of the Earl of Coventry's vast estate; such purposeless structures were called follies. From the tower, it is straight downhill through crowds of jeering sheep into beautiful Broadway.

Broadway's single major street is something of an outdoor museum, with architectural gems lining both sides of the "broadway." Fine antique shops, coffee houses, pubs, boutiques, and hotels constitute a thriving commercial district. Stay a couple of days, explore the villages, and try some of the other suggested walks; the Cotswolds do not fail to delight.

Optional Maps: Landranger 150, 151/Pathfinder 1043

Time/Distance: 2 hours 10 minutes/6 miles (9.6 km)

Difficulties: Some difficult ascents

Toilet Facilities: Chipping Campden, Broadway Tower, Broadway

Refreshments: Chipping Campden, Broadway Tower, Broadway

Getting There: From Broadway take the Cresswell Bus (tel. 01386–48655), which departs from the Swan Hotel, to Chipping Campden. Currently, buses run on Tuesdays, Thursdays, and Saturdays—one in the morning and one in the late afternoon. Schedules are available at the Broadway tourist office. There is also an early-morning Wednesday BusLine (bus #515) service (tel. 01788–535555).

Trail Notes

___ 1a. The bus drops you off at the bus shelter in the center of Chipping Campden. Walk back down the road that the bus entered town on (to your right as you walk through town, there will be the Cotswold House Hotel, the Kings Arms Hotel, and a Midland Bank straight ahead).

___ 1b. When you reach St. Catherine's Church and primary school, turn right. You will see a sign indicating "Cotswold Way." From this point, yellow arrows will guide you out of town.

___ 2a. When you reach an asphalt road, turn left.

___ 2b. After a couple of minutes of walking along the asphalt road, you will turn right into a field where you see the sign indicating "Cotswold Way." Follow the yellow arrows which will guide you through the field.

___ 3a. You will emerge from the field onto an asphalt road where you will turn left (there is no sign here).

___ 3b. When you reach an intersection with another asphalt road, continue straight (you will see a Cotswold Way sign).

___ 3c. Shortly after you pass the intersection, you will turn right off the road where you will see a Cotswold Way" sign.

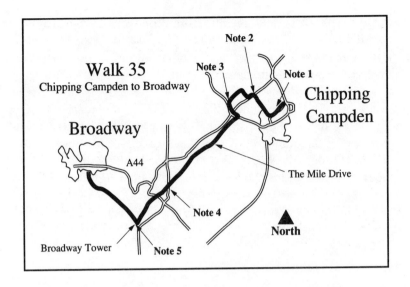

Walk 35
Chipping Campden to Broadway

Broadway

Note 2
Note 3
Note 1
Chipping Campden
A44
The Mile Drive
Note 4
Broadway Tower
Note 5
North

You will parallel the road for a while along what is called "The Mile Drive," but the road soon veers right while you continue straight.

___ 4a. When you come to a road, continue straight ahead into another field. A sign will guide you.

___ 4b. You will soon come to a second road. Cross to the other side, and turn right. You will parallel the road for a short time and then turn left into the woods along a marked route.

___ 5a. From Broadway Tower walk straight downhill along the path into Broadway, which is visible from this point.

___ 5b. Just outside of Broadway, any of the trails to your right will take you into town.

Suggestions for More Walking

The Cotswold Way cuts a scenic path through this most comely part of Britain for 98 miles (158 km) from Bath to Chipping Campden. Kev Reynold's guide *The Cotswold Way*, Cicerone Press, 1990, provides a complete description of the trail. For a longer, equally scenic walk, take the bus from Broadway to Winchcombe, and hike back along the Cotswold Way. Use the above guide or Pathfinder maps 1043 and 1067. Another attractive possibility involves taking the Gloucestershire and Warwickshire steam train from Greet, north of Winchcombe, to the only other stop at Toddington. A trail parallels the tracks until you reach the first road at Didbrook. Pass through this tiny village, join the Cotswold Way at the other end of town, and walk back to Winchcombe, passing through the haunting remains of twelfth-century Hailes Abbey (total 4.5 miles/7.6 km). If you are on a tight schedule, at least take the round-trip walk (total 1.3 miles/2 km) from Broadway to Broadway Tower and back; the views, in all directions, are astonishing.